D0992358

The Self-Regarding Institution: Information for Excellence

About the Author

Peter T. Ewell—Director, since 1981, of the National Center for Higher Education Management Systems [NCHEMS] W. K. Kellogg Foundation project to promote the use of student-outcomes information at seven colleges and universities across the nation . . . 1978-1981, Coordinator for Long-Range Planning, Governors State University . . . developed a student-tracking system for assessing attrition and graduate follow-up; developed a comprehensive data base for academic program review and evaluation of support programs . . . 1975-1978, Harper Fellow in Social Science and Assistant Director of the Public Affairs Program, University of Chicago . . . Ph.D. in Political Science, Yale University, 1976 . . . consultant on program planning and evaluation to the Michigan Council for the Arts, the Ohio Arts Council, Kentucky Arts Commission, Illinois Arts Council, and other public-service agencies . . . 1980, team leader for the National Endowment for the Arts partnership consultation program in Michigan . . . author of numerous policy studies at Governors State as well as articles in academic journals . . . 1981, American Theater Association Theory and Criticism award for "The Conscience of the King: A Socio-Historical Analysis of Erdman's *The Suicide*."

mgen
(Don)

An NCHEMS Executive Overview

The Self-Regarding Institution: Information for Excellence

Peter Ewell

1984

BIBLOTHEQUES

LIBRARIES
University of Ottawa

National Center for Higher Education Management Systems
P.O. Drawer P   Boulder, Colorado 80302
An Affirmative Action / Equal Opportunity Employer

All rights reserved. No part of this publication may be reproduced or transmitted in any form or by any means, electronic or mechanical, including photocopy, recording, or any information storage and retrieval system, without permission in writing from the publisher.

Copyright ©1984 by the National Center for Higher Education Management Systems, Inc.

Published in 1984 in the United States of America by the National Center for Higher Education Management Systems, Inc., Boulder, Colorado 80302.

Printed in the United States of America. This publication was not printed at the expense of the federal government.

Designed by Grant Duncan,
Graphic Directions, Boulder, Colorado

LB
2341
.E87
1984

iv

Contents

Preface

The original draft of this Executive Overview was prepared in April of 1984 for the National Institute of Education Study Group on the Conditions of Excellence in American Higher Education. To further its inquiry, the Study Group needed a document to summarize and organize the many available approaches for defining the outcomes of college and university experiences. Because of their commitment to institutional assessment, members of the Study Group also were interested in discovering promising approaches to using assessment information to improve curriculum, instruction, and management. Preparation of the Study Group paper—originally titled "Dimensions of Excellence in Postsecondary Education"—was supported by a grant from the W. K. Kellogg Foundation. Recommendations on the need for institutional assessment and feedback became integral parts of the Study Group's report, *Involvement in Learning*, which was issued by the Department of Education in October 1984.

In preparing this manuscript I have incurred many debts. Discussions with Study Group members helped clarify many murky ideas; I am particularly grateful to Sandy Astin, Harold Hodgkinson, and Zelda Gamson for their comments and encouragement. Dennis Jones of NCHEMS provided the initial stimulus for the Study Group paper and gave continuing guidance through its many versions. In gathering material on the institutional uses of assessment information, I am particularly grateful to Austin Doherty and Marcia Mentkowski of Alverno College, to Charles McClain and Darrell Krueger of Northeast Missouri State University, to Trudy Banta of the University of Tennessee, Knoxville, and to the campus project directors of the recently completed NCHEMS/Kellogg project on the uses of student-outcomes information. I am also grateful for the editorial assistance of Rolf Norgaard and Sally Furgeson and for the flying fingers of Paula Dressler in preparing the manuscript for publication.

Finally, I wish again to thank the W. K. Kellogg Foundation for its continuing support of efforts to improve colleges and universities through better information. These efforts are indeed having an impact, and it has been a privilege over the past three years to have been a part of them.

Introduction

Calls for improving the quality of our colleges and universities have been increasingly insistent of late. Following hard upon recent inquiries about the condition of elementary and secondary education have been numerous attempts to assess both the objectives and the effect of postsecondary education. More importantly, these assessments are accompanied by rising levels of public uncertainty about the place and worth of higher education in American society. After several decades of unbroken confidence and unprecedented expansion, higher education is now being called upon to demonstrate that it has been making a difference.

Thus has begun a growing movement toward making colleges and universities—particularly in the public sector—more explicitly responsible for demonstrating their educational effectiveness. More and more states, for example, are requiring institutions to engage in formal processes of academic program review (Barak 1982) as concrete evidence of program quality. Furthermore, some states have initiated processes for assessing actual educational outcomes—both for assuring competence among graduating students and for rewarding institutions that can demonstrate effectiveness. Finally, one major recommendation of a recent national panel on attaining excellence in higher education is for colleges and universities to explicitly assess the impacts they are having on students (National Institute of Education 1984).

In the face of such calls for improvement, the response of higher education has been, at best, ambiguous. Many educators argue that the very nature of the higher-education enterprise effectively precludes improvement through increased external accountability. Such positions rely implicitly on the traditional decentralized, self-policing character of the academy to make warranted changes. Opposing positions call for establishing common external standards of accountability. These positions hold that the academy's traditional self-corrective mechanisms, if they ever existed, have broken down. Such positions maintain that higher education's greatest current problem is a crisis of confidence among its constituents, and that the traditional assurances will no longer suffice.

Such tensions are, of course, not unfamiliar in the development of social institutions. Writing 150 years ago in the preface to *Democracy in America*, Alexis de Tocqueville viewed with rising concern the broadening and leveling effects of increased social equality and access. Broadened participation, he noted, brought with it increased general prosperity; its leveling tendencies, however, entailed inevitable threats to quality in many areas— most particularly education, the arts, and public life. As a result of this tension, Tocqueville reports that his inquiry "has been conducted under the impulse of a kind of religious dread," a feeling arising both from the seeming inevitability of the process to which he was a witness and from his profound doubts about its probable consequences.

Calls to increase accountability for educational outcomes should provoke in us analogous feelings of "religious dread." Higher education, too, has undergone profound changes in its structure and characteristics over the past four decades (National Institute of Education 1984). Institutions have become larger, more specialized, and more public. Students have become more varied in background, preparation, and patterns of attendance. Curricula have evolved from the traditional liberal arts to a broad array of occupational, professional, and special-purpose programs. As a result of this diversity, the pattern of higher-education outcomes has become almost bewilderingly complex. Thus, calls for accountability stem, at least in part, from a simple desire on the part of those who support higher education to *understand* what has occurred.

On the one hand, such calls for accountability are a healthy development. In an era of constrained resources and many alternative opportunities for social investment, higher education can no longer afford to base its claims to resources on the self-evidence of its benefits. Indeed, as institutions, students, and curricula have changed, the actual nature of these benefits has become increasingly murky. Traditional proponents of higher education see such benefits from within a time-honored perspective of broad liberal education—a heritage dominated by well-established models of the small college and the comprehensive research university. Consequently, these traditional proponents view the recent proliferation of community colleges and vocational institutions with alarm. Newer advocates of postsecondary education see its benefits in terms of their ability to answer society's need for trained manpower in critical fields. As a result, they view the maintenance of many traditional institutions as an expensive luxury. The situation has not been helped by the fact that the case for higher education has, in its expansionist past, been founded upon both positions, and has therefore involved some rather grandiose claims of effectiveness. What we are now increasingly being asked to demonstrate is nothing more than that for which we in the past have had the hubris to claim credit. Unpleasant as it may be, increased external accountability may force us to make necessary choices among alternative missions and priorities.

Peter Ewell

On the other hand, positions that stress the traditional autonomy of the academic enterprise are equally important. We have learned repeatedly that the practices of teaching and scholarly inquiry are fragile indeed. To be effective, both require an open, participatory environment. Both operate best in the context of a decentralized and "values oriented" institution, one that can isolate itself somewhat from a wider, more instrumental environment. And both flourish only under situations where risk taking is seen as normal and is rewarded. Conformity to external standards, at whatever level such standards are developed or applied, is, in this context, an alien and a counterproductive activity.

This is by no means to say that higher education ought therefore to be unaccountable by *any* standards. The maintenance of standards within individual disciplines constitutes the core of the academic enterprise. Indeed, a first step in creating and maintaining external accountability should be founded upon this fact. *Internal* standard setting and evaluation, a process familiar to us as practicing teachers and scholars, should be made both more generally recognized and more explicit in our institutions.

If there is one generalization that can be made about the academic community, it is that we place unusual value on acquiring information and using it for social and individual improvement. Much of the historic rhetoric of scholarship, for example, emphasizes the role of the university in creating and maintaining society's store of knowledge. Furthermore, such rhetoric asserts that this role is not self-fulfilling. Rather, it is undertaken to improve society's capacity to become more self-regarding and self-improving, to encourage society to recognize its strengths and correct its deficiencies. At the same time, an equally historic aim of higher education—particularly liberal education—is to produce these same self-regarding and self-improving qualities in individual learners. Reverence for exact information and its application to generate new knowledge and to improve practice are those qualities, above all, that we wish to instill in our students. They are also precisely those qualities we seek to exemplify and reward in our disciplinary lives.

Given that we have constructed a culture in higher education that appears so publicly to value information, it is surprising how little of it we tend to have about ourselves. And more surprising is the fact that what we do know about what works and what does not in particular colleges and universities has had but little effect on actual teaching and administration. The reasons for this apparent contradiction are many, some quite legitimate. The central theme of this Executive Overview is that to achieve excellence in the diverse activities currently comprising postsecondary education, we must create explicit, institution-specific mechanisms for regularly assessing the degree to which we are in fact attaining our collective goals.

Such mechanisms are fast becoming hallmarks of what can be termed the self-regarding institution. Like the traditional small college, the self-regarding institution is aware of its distinctiveness, its purposes, and its strengths and its deficiencies. Furthermore, like the small college, it has ways of structuring a dialogue about itself that is carried on by all of its members. Most important of all, discussions of effectiveness in the self-regarding institution are *informed* discussions. Indeed, they are based upon explicit and available collective information about what students at the institution are experiencing, and information about the linkages between various aspects of the institution's program and particular aspects of student growth and development.

In most cases, however, current modes of organization in higher education continue little changed from the time when these impacts and linkages were directly observable by the academic community. In the environment of the small, private liberal-arts college or the elite research university, a network of shared values and implicit communication tends automatically to keep issues of educational practice—its ends and its effectiveness— at the forefront of institutional discussion. In such a context, there is little need for explicit, structured information about how the institution is faring. And indeed, in some of our best institutions these processes of value building and tacit communication remain vigorous and effective.

For the majority of current postsecondary institutions, however, these traditional self-assessment mechanisms are not present. Nor, despite recent calls to return to them (Martin 1982), are such mechanisms operationally feasible. The large public university, regional service institution, or community college is simply too big and too multicultural, inhabited by too many student clienteles, and responsible to too many diverse constituencies to allow such implicit mechanisms for self-assessment. The challenge to administration in such situations is to create explicit, information-based structures of incentives and accountability to replace our more traditional implicit methods of self-assessment and self-improvement.

Such systems can revitalize our institutions in much the same manner as traditional academic dialogue. Certainly, they must be constructed to be consistent with local institutional values and sensibilities. But they also have the potential to reassure critical external constituencies—increasingly dissatisfied with higher education's silence on the question of effectiveness—that we are demonstrably concerned with achieving institutional excellence and that we have visibly committed ourselves to its assessment and improvement.

Still, the desired ends of postsecondary education remain diverse and largely incommensurable. This poses an obstacle to establishing outcomes-oriented assessment mechanisms. Clearly, different kinds of higher-education institutions are in vastly different businesses and ought, therefore, to be held accountable for different things. Equally clear, however, is the demand that all institutions produce certified graduates with an assured level of basic or professional skill. Both objectives are legitimate, but they are difficult to discuss because as yet we have no common language that systematically distinguishes the several dimensions of postsecondary educational outcomes. In practice, this causes some important misunderstandings. Is "educational outcome," for example, to refer to actual *changes* in student knowledge or abilities resulting from the learning process, regardless of the ultimate knowledge or skill level attained? Or is it rather to refer to the *actual level* of attainment at the end of the process, regardless of the level at which the student began? The current controversy over "value added" assessment is generated in large part by the conviction that we must judge institutional quality in terms of one of these criteria but not both. We could avoid much of this confusion by recognizing that both notions are appropriate, but for different analytical and assessment purposes.

Equally daunting for institutions attempting to establish comprehensive self-assessment programs are the multiple, often highly complex, ways educational researchers have chosen to structure the particular outcomes of postsecondary education. Each such structure has its virtues. Each provides a set of dimensions or categories well suited to a particular type of institution or method of analysis. But the majority of such conceptual schemes are relatively inaccessible and of limited use to the practicing academic administrator.

The objective of part 1 of this book, therefore, is to summarize and organize these conceptual efforts and present them in such a way that some clear institutional choices can be made. An administrator needs to know which of many possible outcomes dimensions are important and where, as a result, to focus an institutional-assessment effort.

Establishing such an effort, however, requires a substantial reorientation of the way institutions of higher education typically do business. As in the elementary or secondary setting, the process of producing better "outputs" from higher education is a function of the classroom, of the students who inhabit it, of the curriculum, and of the learning environment. We in higher education certainly know less than we should about the explicit linkages between such factors and particular kinds of student learning outcomes.

Peter Ewell

But we often know more than act upon. What is generally lacking in postsecondary classrooms is not intellectual talent but a consistent set of institutional incentives to use this talent effectively. Creating such a set of institutional incentives is an administrative task. It is not enough for us to know more about the probable linkages between learning factors and learning outcomes. To achieve excellence in the fragmented, organizationally conservative setting of the college or university, we must also know how to induce institutions to build the necessary kinds of institutional commitments and make the kinds of structural changes required.

A second purpose of this book, therefore, is demonstrative: to provide evidence of the ways institutions have actually *used* assessments of student growth and development to make improvements in instruction, in curriculum, and in the student learning environment. Part 2 of the volume offers evidence about institutional experience with explicit institutional assessment. In most cases, the research supporting these initial efforts has been both unsystematic and technically unsophisticated. In all cases, the need for more and better research about the postsecondary learning process has been an important product of the utilization effort. But the biggest payoffs have occurred because of the effort itself. Adopting an explicit program for assessing and improving educational outcomes requires an institution to articulate and internalize a special kind of collective responsibility.

Based upon evidence from a number of such institutions, two important arguments can be made. First, it is quite possible for individual institutions to undertake such efforts without a massive infusion of external resources. What campuses require is primarily an integration and reorganization of numerous existing student-assessment activities. Secondly, the effectiveness of such efforts is highly dependent upon their being institution-specific and participatory in character. Neither government nor the research community can hope to impose solutions—no matter how well informed—if faculty and administrators have not first internalized the logic of these solutions through their own evaluations and experiences.

The two purposes of this book, though distinct, remain highly related. Institutional efforts to achieve excellence must first be informed by an attempt to *define* excellence from within the distinctive environment and perspective of each institution. They must secondly be grounded in an attempt to *assess* the attainment of excellence through an explicit, systematic, and participatory examination of educational outcomes. In defining what it wants its students to be, a college or university essentially defines itself. In assessing the degree to which educational goals have actually been achieved, a college or university identifies critical areas for future action. Self-definition and self-examination constitute the first and most important steps toward ongoing self-improvement. In the absence of these steps, it is impossible to conceive of achieving excellence.

PART 1

Structuring Excellence: Dimensions of Outcomes

Excellence in higher education, as in anything else, is a concept difficult to define yet difficult to disagree with. Lack of consensus about the concept is heavily bound up with its lack of clarity; every attempt to define its attributes is likely to increase the disagreement. Indeed, the notion of excellence seems to contain an essential contradiction. Its very construction connotes exclusivity: to be "excellent" is to be distinctive, superior, and worthy of emulation. Excellence thus establishes an external standard that, by definition, not all will meet. Yet failure to strive for excellence—in business, in sport, or in intellectual attainment—is considered, especially in American society, an abdication responsibility. Quite aside from the imposed standard, working toward excellence is, in itself, a valued process—a process by which individuals and institutions attempt to move themselves from where they currently are to where they and others would like them to be.

So, is excellence a standard or a process? This conceptual contradiction is particularly imbedded in discussions of the excellence of postsecondary education and of the institutions that provide it. On the one hand, excellence is judged in terms of particular sets of standards: available resources, the structure of programs and curricula, and the intellectual characteristics and attainments of faculty and students. (This theme has been particularly evident in the process of postsecondary accreditation.) On the other hand, these sets of standards are taken to be indicative of an underlying process. High levels of resources, well-structured programs, and an able faculty and student body are assumed to be highly correlated with educational growth. They are consequently valued largely because of the perceived increments of educational growth they are believed to produce.

So long as most higher-education institutions were essentially in the same business, the terms of this contradiction remained obscure. The appropriate outcomes of higher education were relatively few and well agreed upon: a liberal education, with its associated value structure, and scholarly attainment within a particular discipline. Furthermore, the production function associated with these outcomes, though relatively unexamined, was comparatively straightforward: a four-year curriculum, built around a disciplinary major, offered to a small and carefully selected body of recent high-school graduates.

All of this now has changed. New institutions with new missions have been established, and many others have seen their missions redefined. Added to this have been vast increases in higher-education participation rates over the past three decades. Legitimate outcomes of higher education are now claimed in many different arenas, and the educational processes used by different types of institutions to produce these outcomes vary in the extreme. Under such circumstances, defining the concept of excellence in higher education, either as a standard or as a process of educational growth, presents a considerable challenge. To do so within the confines of a single traditional dimension of educational outcomes is impossible.

STRUCTURING EXCELLENCE

Given this complexity, the main purpose of part 1 of this book is to provide a consistent language for discussing the outcomes of postsecondary education. The argument will be that institutions achieve excellence in postsecondary education insofar as they produce demonstrable changes along particular dimensions of educational outcomes consistent with (1) institutional objectives, (2) student educational goals, and (3) the expressed needs of society and of particular constituencies within society. An important distinction in this argument will be between the *empirical content* of the particular changes produced (a question of measurement and educational technology) and the *values placed upon* these changes by different interested parties in the system (a question of perspective and preference).

The implications of this discussion for the accountability of higher-education institutions are many. Posing multiple dimensions of educational outcomes and recognizing the legitimacy of many perspectives on the valuation of these outcomes at first may seem to deny totally the notion of institutional accountability. Clearly, from this point of view, ranking all institutions in terms of a single set of evaluative criteria will be impossible. But the existence of both multiple outcomes dimensions and multiple perspectives on the value of particular outcomes may yield new, more useful ways to demonstrate accountability for excellence. Such an approach, for example, suggests that all institutions should be held accountable (1) for clearly stating what kinds of outcomes they are trying to produce, (2) for explicitly assessing the degree to which they are attaining these outcomes, and (3) for making appropriate changes to improve the situation where the data warrant. Such an approach also implies that groups within society with a need for particular educational products have an obligation both to state that need clearly and in outcomes terms, and to be able to apply a rigorous and consistent set of assessment standards.

Peter Ewell

The chapters making up part 1 approach these issues from several directions. The first, "Educational Excellence as a Change Concept," is intended to clarify some important distinctions between the ways we typically talk about educational excellence. On the one hand, we often view educational excellence in terms of absolute levels of attainment; on the other, we often view excellence in terms of the degree to which students change as a result of the learning experience. And for both of these, we tend to confuse the issue of whether attainment or change has occurred, which is an empirical question, with how we and others feel about it, which is a question of valuation.

The second chapter, "Some Different Perspectives on Educational Outcomes," reviews major elements of the literature on college and university outcomes. This literature is vast and diverse, and the studies it comprises were intended for many different purposes. The purpose of the chapter is to integrate these various approaches and set the stage for developing a common institutional language for describing such outcomes.

The third chapter, "A Classification of Outcomes Dimensions," presents the resulting structure along four major dimensions: knowledge, skills, attitudes/values, and relationships with society. An intent of the classification is to indicate clearly the differences among different types of educational outcomes, and to emphasize that different institutions can legitimately pursue excellence along different dimensions. Nevertheless—as the fourth chapter argues—various constituencies within society will value achievements on each of these dimensions differently. And institutions ignore such external valuation at their peril. Indeed, much of the content of strategic planning, currently in vogue in higher education, consists of matching an array of external valuations with a defined set of internal capacities and potential capacities to produce particular types of outcomes.

It is a reasonable question to ask, of course, why it is necessary to pay attention to the issues at all. If many potential impacts of colleges and universities are possible, and if all are legitimate, a language that distinguishes them may seem superfluous. Furthermore, the extensive literature on college impact would seem to provide ample justification for almost any course of action a particular institution might wish to pursue. Despite these arguments, our current lack of a systematic way of talking about educational quality, and about the different directions along which it can be sought, is a growing obstacle to both individual and systemic improvement.

At the systemic level, lack of a good vocabulary on educational outcomes has led to considerable confusion in recent public debates about the merits of particular postsecondary educational systems. Much recent criticism of community colleges, for example, has been based upon the relatively low degree production and high attrition rates typical of such institutions. Because these institutions have not been defined in outcomes terms, most of the right questions in this debate have simply not been asked— questions regarding the ability of former students to perform in an employment skills area, or to benefit from personal self-development, or to transfer successfully to a senior institution.

Indeed, it is important to recognize that most of the major developments in the landscape of higher education over the past three decades have been additive rather than homogeneous. New clienteles have largely been accommodated in new institutions with new programs and missions, leaving many established institutions essentially unchanged. However, public discussion of these changes has, almost exclusively, proceeded as though such changes *were* homogeneous—that all institutions will be affected equally by the same demographic trends, shifts in societal manpower needs, and so on. Much of this confusion, it may be argued, has been due to our own inability to articulate clearly, in outcomes terms, what the major differences are.

At the institutional level, the need for such a language is equally apparent. Recent studies of institutional decline have emphasized the importance of an institution's ability to state clearly its particular mission and the particular types of students it intends to produce. In Chaffee's study of eight small private liberal-arts colleges, for example, those institutions that successfully recovered possessed this ability; simultaneously, they adapted their programs to changing societal demand. Those that did not possess this ability continued to decline despite their many efforts to adapt to serve new needs and new clienteles (Chaffee 1984). The general principle is apparent: educational institutions, like other collective enterprises, cannot hope to achieve excellence unless they can effectively communicate to others the particular business they are in. Doing so requires development of a common language centered not around the resources they possess or the reputation they have achieved, but on what they, in fact, expect and hope to produce.

CHAPTER 1

Educational Excellence as a Change Concept

I n applying the concept of excellence to education, the same term is generally used to refer both to the product of an educational experience and to the experience itself. Assessment of these two, however, is likely to be radically different. While products may be evaluated by reference to a static external standard, processes can only be judged in terms of the *changes* that occur as a result. Such a distinction between product and process evaluation is, of course, rarely achieved in practice. Some educational products are indeed commonly assessed in process or "value added" terms—for example, continuing education or professional development. Similarly, some processes are generally assessed in terms of standards—for example, the standards of curriculum structure that are used as part of many professional accreditation processes.

For the most part, however, the evaluation of educational product and educational process are appropriately distinct activities. However, both activities share the same measurement technologies. Also, the results of measurement or assessment are presented in terms of the same units. A given test or assessment procedure may, for instance, be applied to ascertain a particular student's level of development at a single point in time. At this point, an appropriate question may be asked about the degree to which the result of this measurement corresponds to a previously established standard. Alternatively, the same test or procedure may be administered over time to ascertain the amount of development resulting from the educational process. At this point, an appropriate question may be asked about the differences between a measurement taken at the beginning of the process and one taken at its conclusion. Both measurement procedures, in order to be meaningful, involve comparisons, but the points of reference differ notably.

More importantly, the *motives* for comparison are quite different. The primary reason for comparing the results of a measurement procedure to a particular standard is to place a value on the product. Many quite different standards may in this way be applied to identical outcomes, and the judgments of worth entailed will, as a result, be quite different. The primary reason, on the other hand, for comparing measurement results at the beginning and end of a particular process is to ascertain whether a particular change has, in fact, taken place. This is a purely empirical question and does not automatically involve valuation of the outcome. Furthermore, in contrast to the valuation process, such a procedure should result in only one right answer.

In the face of these issues, making conceptual sense of the notion of excellence in higher education means being clear about two basic distinctions. The first is between assessing the actual changes occurring as a result of the educational process (an empirical measurement question) and making judgments about the results of the process (a process of valuation). The second distinction is between alternative ways of making evaluative judgments. As figure 1 illustrates, any conceptual treatment of excellence requires that these distinctions be approached in the proper order.

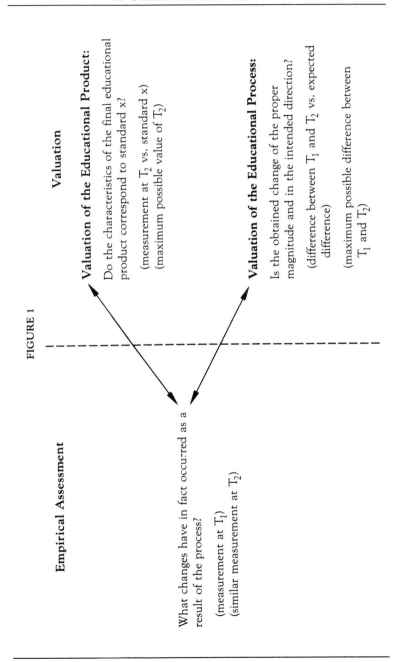

FIGURE 1

Empirical Assessment

What changes have in fact occurred as a result of the process?

(measurement at T_1)
(similar measurement at T_2)

Valuation

Valuation of the Educational Product:

Do the characteristics of the final educational product correspond to standard x?

(measurement at T_2 vs. standard x)
(maximum possible value of T_2)

Valuation of the Educational Process:

Is the obtained change of the proper magnitude and in the intended direction?

(difference between T_1 and T_2 vs. expected difference)

(maximum possible difference between T_1 and T_2)

Peter Ewell

Measurement vs. Valuation

The most important initial distinction is between the processes of measurement and valuation. Primary activities in the measurement process include establishing appropriate categories and units for measurement, and applying these categories to an array of available data about the phenomenon to be measured. In principle, neither the choice of categories nor the application process is a value-driven process. In practice, of course, we tend to choose the categories in terms of an implied valuation scheme; this tendency accounts for many of the variations among schemes that classify educational outcomes.

Regardless of its origins, once such a set of outcomes dimensions or categories is in place, it can be applied to many different situations and at many points in time. The resulting outcomes profiles can then be compared in many ways. Exiting students from different types of institutions or in different types of programs, for example, will undoubtedly differ in significant ways. Similarly, important differences will be found in the characteristics of entering students from various backgrounds and with various aspirations. Many such comparisons of student profiles are possible given the purposes of any empirical investigation. To understand the actual effects of a given instructional process, however, only one type of comparison *must* be accomplished: that between student profiles at the beginning of the process and at its conclusion. More importantly, only the comparison between before and after will provide the kind of information needed to intervene in and improve the educational process.

Two Kinds of Valuation

A quite different set of activities is typical of any valuation process. Here the primary object is to assess a given student profile—however obtained—in terms of a valued external standard.

Many types of standards may be appropriate for particular purposes, and the application of such standards to the same empirical profile will yield quite different results. But all such valuations of educational outcomes can be grouped essentially into two classes.

The first set of standards is static and is applied to the student on exit. The essential question posed by this type of valuation is one of certification—the degree to which the educational product, as currently assessed, is consistent with a desired level of attainment. Within this conception, educational excellence can be defined in several ways. One approach maximizes the proportion of graduates meeting the standard on completion of the program. An alternative notion of excellence might involve attainment of the maximum possible score, in excess of the standard.

The second set of standards is applied to the actual educational gains experienced as a result of instruction. The essential question posed by this type of valuation is one of educational effectiveness—the degree to which particular gains have been achieved consistent with objectives. Here again, excellence can be defined in several ways. One approach is the proportion of students for whom minimum acceptable gains on particular valued dimensions are achieved. An alternative approach defines excellence in terms of the maximum possible gains obtained, consistent with previously defined instructional objectives.

A Working Definition of Quality in Educational Outcomes

A major assumption in this chapter's discussion is that higher education can only be meaningfully conceptualized as a change process. The notion of an "educational outcome" is thus also a change concept—the assessed differences in the attributes and abilities of a student upon leaving the process as compared with those upon entering the process. Instruction changes some *concrete attributes*, and these changes are, at least in principle, measurable. But instruction in itself does nothing to change the *value* of these attributes—changed or unchanged—to different segments of society.

Within this general framework, a working definition of instructional quality might look something like the following:

> Quality in educational outcomes is attained when the greatest net gains in particular student attributes and abilities from entry to exit, as assessed along a set of defined dimensions, are accomplished (1) consistent with previously set institutional instructional objectives, and (2) consistent with an appropriate array of values placed upon these gains by particular constituencies (including students) within society.

Operationalizing this definition first requires, then, proposal of an appropriate general set of dimensions along which to array concrete educational outcomes. Secondly, typical arrays of values placed upon these dimensions by different segments of society must be identified and reconciled with particular patterns of concrete outcomes. These activities are the concern of chapters 2 through 4.

CHAPTER 2

Some Different Perspectives on Educational Outcomes

A ttempts to structure the outcomes of postsecondary education have been many and varied (Lenning 1977b). Some, like Astin's fourfold typology, have been developed to support particular research efforts (Astin, Panos, and Creager 1967). Others, like Harshman's taxonomy of student outcomes (1979), Bloom's taxonomy of cognitive objectives (1956), or Chickering's "vectors" of student development (1969), have been constructed to summarize and inventory the results of a broader field of inquiry. Still others, like Lenning's "outcomes structures for postsecondary education," result from attempts to build a common language for institutional data exchange (Lenning 1977a).

Each of these structures was designed for a particular purpose, and their characteristics reflect their different purposes. Each therefore possesses important limitations when applied outside its original conceptual environment. Those taxonomies designed to support and inventory research, for example, often classify as much by source of data as by conceptual category. Those designed as standards for communicating institutional data are often alarmingly static and take little account of the complex causal interactions among outcomes elements. But for the most part, it is clear that those who have tried to map the territory of postsecondary educational outcomes have been viewing the same landscape.

Our purpose in once again exploring this common conceptual territory is not simply to add to a growing list of overlapping classifications and descriptions. Rather, it is to determine some of the common elements underlying all such classifications and then to use these common elements to propose a set of relatively independent dimensions of excellence in postsecondary education. A second purpose is to propose these dimensions not as static standards for evaluation but as distinct elements of potential student growth and development.

Cognitive Development

One way of beginning the process of classifying higher-education outcomes is to examine briefly a number of distinct traditions of student-development research. The first, and oldest, tradition is cognitive, involving the processes and correlates of individual student learning. Summative assessments of cognitive gain in a college environment go back as far as 1928 to the Pennsylvania General College Tests (Learned and Wood 1938). Experimental work in the classroom—drawing heavily on learning theories developed for elementary and secondary education—has at least as long a history (Lenning and Munday 1974; Feldman and Newcomb 1969). And indeed, assessment of cognitive development has become, in the past two decades, a major industry (see the review in Pace 1979). Commercial testing instruments, now a prominent part of the postsecondary landscape, are used in functions as diverse as admissions, placement, and professional certification. Increasingly, such assessments have become part of discussions of institutional accountability as well.

DIFFERENT PERSPECTIVES

The underlying question of all research in the cognitive tradition concerns the process of acquiring concrete knowledge—either general knowledge or knowledge of a particular area of study. The unit of analysis for most of this work has been the individual student, although often as a member of a particular population—traditional, minority, or adult. And a major intent has been development of new instructional technologies—curricular structures, learning environments, and presentational methods or formats.

Impacts upon Society

A second tradition of academic investigation involves the impacts of postsecondary instruction upon society as revealed through patterns of employment, social mobility, and social behavior. Investigations of postgraduate experience for particular institutions can be traced back to the mid-1930s (Eurich and Pace 1938; Greenleaf 1939). Attempts to bring these studies together to form a more comprehensive picture of the societal impact on higher education are, however, much more recent (Bowen 1977). Indeed, many such investigations are at least partially due to mounting public concern with the historical "return on investment" of an increasingly costly public higher-education enterprise.

Research questions in this tradition have been generally more diffuse than in the cognitive domain. One set of questions concerns the congruence between the knowledge and skills provided by higher education, and the needs for such knowledge and skills in society. This can be either investigated directly for particular industries or interest groups or inferred by the success of graduates in particular fields finding employment and moving upward along a career path. A second set of questions has to do with effective social functioning. This concerns the role of higher education in providing basic skills such as problem solving, critical thinking,

Peter Ewell

and information gathering important to a broad range of social activities (for example, Spaeth and Greeley 1970). A third set has to do with the actual changes in social behavior that are assumed to follow from such skills. Examples of such changes include enhanced political and community participation, increased tolerance for cultural diversity, and different approaches to marital roles and child rearing (for example, the reviews in Pace 1974). Within this tradition, the impacts of higher education on individuals are not manifested within the individuals, but rather in terms of changes in the *relationships* between individuals and particular groups in society.

The College Experience

A third tradition of academic investigation explores the broader psychological and attitudinal impact of college on those who experience it. Rather than being confined to cognitive development, such studies examine the development, in the course of education, of the "whole person"—attitudes, perceptions, values, and the interactions of these elements (for example, Chickering 1969). Investigation within this tradition has not been limited to the production of such changes within the college environment. It has also covered the persistence of such changes after graduation or withdrawal (Trent and Medsker 1968; Newcomb, Koenig, Flacks, and Warwick 1967).

Research questions in this tradition generally focus upon the kinds of changes in attitudes, perceptions, and behavior that actually occur in the course of the educational experience. Such questions also emphasize the degree to which such changes can be linked to explicit characteristics of the campus or educational environment (for example, Astin 1977). The unit of analysis for research, as in the cognitive tradition, is the individual student. Also as in the cognitive tradition, there is often an explicit focus on action: how can we make appropriate changes in campus learning environments designed to produce the kinds of "identities" we would most like to see (Astin 1979)? And finally, like that of the cognitive tradition, the vast majority of this work concentrates on the development of the 18- to 21-year-old student in a structured, residential, four-year undergraduate curriculum.

This third tradition covers from a different perspective some of the same questions addressed by the research tradition that focuses on societal impact. The development of particular clusters of attitudes and values is often identified with the acquisition of broad classes of social-functioning skills—for example, Chickering's seven "vectors of development" (1969), or more narrowly within the college experience itself, Pace's notion of "quality of student effort" (1984). In this sense, a strong concern of this third tradition is the production of particular, needed "metaskills," presumed to be of value to both the individual and society.

Occupational Skills

A final, fourth tradition of investigation is much more recent and narrowly focused. It consists of a large number of institution- and program-specific studies on the effectiveness of vocational and applied skills programs in providing training relevant to the needs of particular occupations and industries (see, for example, the review of proprietary institutions in Trivett 1974). The unit of analysis for such investigations is generally the program being assessed; the primary research question, the degree to which the program has provided students with enhanced abilities to perform particular, well-defined tasks in the workplace. A few such studies rely upon independent assessments of particular skills through an explicit testing or demonstration process. The majority, however, rely upon reports of enhanced effectiveness from particular employers, or from students and former students.

In marked contrast to the other three traditions, such investigations have rarely taken place in the context of the four-year undergraduate institution. Rather, they have been conducted by and for two-year occupational programs resident in public community colleges, corporate training programs, and other proprietary settings.

The Need for Multiple Dimensions

While the overlap among these four traditions of investigation is considerable, each appears to cover a relatively distinct dimension of educational impact. Certainly, the case for an independent cognitive dimension seems indisputable, and virtually all attempts to structure educational outcomes have broken out this element as distinctive. Similarly, there seems a clear case with the fourth tradition for treating the acquisition of particular applicable skills as an outcome element different from the cognitive. The development of attitudes, perceptions, and values addressed by the third tradition, on the other hand, is a good deal more complex. Proponents of this tradition, indeed, would probably subsume cognitive growth and skills development within the broader context of developing personal identity. Nevertheless, there is certainly something distinctive here, and most taxonomies of outcomes rightly contain an independent cognitive dimension. Finally, investigations of the second tradition seem to cut across all categories of knowledge, skills, and attitude, paying special attention to the explicit ways such categories tend to promote or enhance particular relationships between the individual and society. This, too, seems worthy of independent consideration.

The above discussion suggests that a useful way to structure the broad dimensions of postsecondary educational outcomes is in terms of the diagram presented in figure 2. The essence of this scheme consists of three major dimensions—knowledge, skills,

FIGURE 2

Major Dimensions of Postsecondary Educational Outcomes

- Knowledge

- Skills

- Attitudes/Values

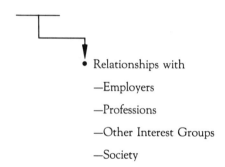

- Relationships with

    —Employers

    —Professions

    —Other Interest Groups

    —Society

and attitudes—accompanied by the manifestation of these dimensions in the subsequent relationships between students and particular groups in society. While each element of this structure needs further exploration, several observations seem relevant at this point.

First, the correspondence between this perspective and a number of previous ways of classifying outcomes is considerable. Knowledge, skills, and attitudes are quite similar, for example, to "cognitive learning, affective development, and practical competence," Bowen's classification of the goals of education (1977). Astin's fourfold typology (Astin, Panos, and Creager 1967) combines knowledge and skills in a single "cognitive" dimension, but his distinction between "psychological" and "behavioral" sources of data about outcomes seems similar to the distinction between individual and "relational" manifestations of the three major outcomes dimensions. The proposed structure also covers more succinctly the categories listed under "human characteristics outcomes" of the NCHEMS Structure for the Outcomes of Post-secondary Education (Lenning 1977a). Chickering's seven vectors of student development represent a quite different approach (1969); many of Chickering's dimensions, however, can be seen as interactions among the proposed elements—particularly those dealing with general social functioning.

More importantly, the categories proposed are not tied to a particular institutional perspective. One difficulty with many inventories is their implicit exclusion of certain types of institutions or student bodies—most notably, vocationally oriented institutions and nontraditional, adult, part-time student bodies. Such institutions and students certainly can be accommodated in almost any classification scheme. In most, however, they appear as exceptions to the dominant traditional four-year-undergraduate center of gravity.

Each of these dimensions will be more fully categorized and discussed in the following chapter.

CHAPTER 3

A Classification of Outcomes Dimensions

An initial task in achieving excellence in educational outcomes is to define the distinct dimensions along which explicit improvements can be attained. Each such dimension can be conceived of as a "vector" of development: a continuum along which individual student changes can be charted and assessed. Different institutions will put different values on changes accomplished along each of these dimensions. Liberal-arts colleges, for example, may emphasize attainment of general knowledge and the acquisition of basic intellectual skills. Community colleges and proprietary institutions may stress mastery of particular kinds of specialized knowledge and vocational skills. And many institutions with a particular religious or values orientation may add to these dimensions student growth in particular areas of attitudinal or moral development.

Each institution will, in essence, construct a series of profiles on the basis of these dimensions. One such profile, the "educational objective" profile, documents the ideal level of attainment of the institution's graduates. In contrast, a second profile documents the actual results obtained, based on assessment of graduating students. A third profile—obtained for entering students—constitutes a baseline for value-added assessment. Explicitly or implicitly, all colleges and universities construct such profiles in order to plan and evaluate educational programs. A major goal of the classification scheme presented in this chapter is to provide a common vocabulary for making such activities as explicit and precise as possible.

The basic structure of the classification scheme is based upon the three dimensions of educational outcomes noted at the end of the last chapter. Student changes in state are assessed in terms of knowledge, skills, and attitudinal/value outcomes. A fourth "dimension" is provided by the many behavioral changes occurring in relationships between students and other elements of society resulting from the educational process. Table 1 summarizes the classification scheme. Each dimension is discussed more fully in the following sections.

Knowledge Outcomes

Knowledge outcomes represent the purely cognitive aspect of educational outcomes. They may be distinguished from skills in a number of ways. The most straightforward such distinction is probably Lenning's (1977a): knowledge consists of familiarity with and analysis and comprehension of facts and principles resident in a particular discipline or field of study, while skills enhance the performance of specific behavioral tasks.

Student gains with respect to knowledge are usefully treated in terms of two broad headings: general knowledge and knowledge of specific fields of study. Widely recognized in extant taxonomies, this distinction is also being used in at least one statewide performance evaluation of higher-education institutions (Bogue 1982).

CLASSIFICATION

TABLE 1

A Classification of Outcomes Dimensions

I. Knowledge Outcomes

    A. General Knowledge (Breadth of Knowledge)
    B. Knowledge of Specific Fields (Depth of Knowledge)

II. Skills Outcomes

    A. General Competence (Social-Functioning) Skills
    B. Professional/Occupational Skills

III. Attitude/Value Outcomes

    A. Personal Goals and Aspirations
    B. General Attitudes, Values, and Satisfactions
    C. Attitudes toward Self (Development of Identity)
    D. Attitudes toward Others

IV. Relationships with Society and with Particular Constituencies

    A. Relationships with Educational Institutions
    B. Relationships with Employers/Industries
    C. Relationships with Professions
    D. Relationships with Family/Community/Society

General Knowledge (Breadth of Knowledge)

General knowledge consists of familiarity with and analysis and comprehension of facts and principles inherent in broad areas of study. Such broad areas will generally contain the traditional divisions of academic study: the humanities, fine arts, physical sciences, and social sciences. Mastery of general knowledge is also generally held to include the ability to relate concepts drawn from different fields as well as to manipulate such concepts effectively, aware of both their analytical potential and their conceptual limits. Senior or College Honors examinations in four-year liberal-arts colleges commonly consist of assessments of this kind. Standardized attempts to measure this attribute include the UAP Area Examinations and the ACT-COMP examination (Forrest 1982; Forrest and Steele 1978).

A list of the component parts of general knowledge might include:

- recall and comprehension of facts in broad areas of study
- recall and comprehension of theories and terminology in broad areas of study
- recall and comprehension of investigative principles and methods in broad areas of study
- recall and comprehension of the history and development of broad areas of study
- ability to relate/integrate approaches and concepts drawn from more than one broad area of study

Knowledge of Specific Fields (Depth of Knowledge)

Knowledge of a specific field requires mastery of the accepted body of facts, theories, language, and techniques of that particular field of study. Such knowledge is most commonly organized within established academic disciplines. In addition to mastery of the subject matter, acquisition of such knowledge will commonly include familiarity with appropriate standards of inquiry embedded in a particular disciplinary culture. Assessments of specific knowledge are abundant in colleges and universities but are generally (and often appropriately) unstandardized. Examples of standardized assessments include the Graduate Record Examinations (GRE) Field Examinations and the College Board/ETS Advanced Placement Examinations.

A partial list of the components that reflect knowledge of a specific field would include:

- recall and comprehension of facts in a particular discipline or specialized field
- recall and comprehension of theories and terminology in a particular discipline or specialized field
- recall and comprehension of investigative principles and methods in a particular discipline or specialized field
- recall and comprehension of the history and development of a particular discipline or specialized field
- ability to effectively manipulate appropriate concepts, theories, and investigative methods to create new knowledge in a particular discipline or specialized field

Skills Outcomes

Skills outcomes consist of the relative abilities of students to perform explicit tasks. Some skills, particularly "academic" skills, will be strongly correlated with particular clusters of knowledge outcomes. Others, such as analytical/problem-solving skills, cut across specific knowledge areas and represent new areas of application. Still others, such as particular occupational skills, are entirely outside the traditional academic arena.

In general, two kinds of skills outcomes are widely recognized. The first consists of skills associated with general competence (often associated with basic social functioning). The second involves the particular specialized and applied skills associated with individual professions and occupations.

General Competence (Social-Functioning) Skills

General competence skills encompass the abilities to use knowledge, organize information, define problems, and discover and implement solutions to problems. The range of components included under this heading is drawn from many parts of previous taxonomies of educational outcomes. Most commonly, the traits described as general competence have been treated as elements of general knowledge. As *applied* elements, however, they are, in many ways, quite different from other elements of general knowledge.

It is interesting to note that most public calls for improvement of the elementary and secondary educational product refer to this cluster of elements rather than to an increase in knowledge per se. Up to now, however, explicit, systematic assessments of general social-functioning skills have been relatively rare. However, some standardized assessment instruments designed to measure elements of this dimension currently do exist. Among these, the ACT-COMP examination, now in widespread use to evaluate general education, actually assesses this dimension much more effectively than it does general knowledge.

A partial list of the components of this dimension would include:

- verbal skills, including reading, reading comprehension, writing, and oral communication
- quantitative skills, including mathematics, statistics, and computing
- leadership/organizational/human-relations skills
- analytical skills, including skills of problem definition, problem solving, and critical thinking
- invention/innovation/creative-thinking skills
- aesthetic-appreciation/creative-expression skills
- physical/motor skills

Professional/Occupational Skills

These skills consist of the particular, specialized skills needed for effective performance in an identified profession or occupation and are most effectively organized in terms of professions and occupations. The distinction between professional and occupational skills is primarily one of level. Occupational skills will likely consist of specific task competencies: for example, the ability to assemble and disassemble machinery, or the ability to operate equipment. Professional skills, on the other hand, consist of particular aggregations of general social-functioning and problem-solving skills appropriate to a given profession. Occupations may be described in standard industrial classification terms. Professions may be described in terms of recognized, generally certifiable career areas, such as engineering, medicine, business, teaching, and particular areas of social service.

Attitude/Value Outcomes

Attitude/value outcomes consist of the affective impacts of the postsecondary educational experience. Types of affective impacts vary from specific, identified satisfactions and dissatisfactions with elements of the college experience on the one hand, to the development and persistence of complete, structured value systems on the other. Indeed, as noted in chapter 2, some outcomes classifications are completely made up of dimensions within this general area. In such approaches, knowledge and skills outcomes are subsumed under more general headings of the development of identity and a personal value structure (for example, Chickering 1969).

Because of the wide range of topics covered, any list of subheadings within this dimension is bound to be arbitrary. Previous classifications appear to cluster around four main types of affective outcomes: personal goals and aspirations, general value systems, attitudes toward self, and attitudes toward others. Each is described briefly below.

Personal Goals and Aspirations

Goals and aspirations are defined in terms of levels, patterns, and directions of personal interests, desires, drives, and ambitions. They may be narrow or broad, long-term or short-term, deeply held or casual. In many cases, these will be career or life-style goals. In other, more narrow cases, they may include goals for further education and lifelong learning.

Assessing such goals as a part of the investigation of educational outcomes is important for at least two reasons, one substantive and the other methodological. The substantive reason is that many educational philosophies consciously seek to transform personal goals as part of the instructional process. The methodological reason for assessing goals is to make better sense of particular patterns of student behavior—for instance, the decision to withdraw from an instructional program without completion of a degree. Measurement options for the assessment of student goals are considerable and include a wide range of standardized psychological-assessment instruments. If goals are defined more narrowly in terms of career choice and motive for further education, most standardized student-opinion questionnaires cover this ground adequately.

A list of the components of this dimension might include:

- general goals and aspirations (life-style, social mobility, family goals, personal goals)
- occupational and career goals
- educational goals
- motivation and drive levels for each of the above

General Attitudes, Values, and Satisfactions

General attitudes and values can be examined both in terms of their extent and content and in terms of their structure. One important objective of many educational programs is to expand the content and sophistication of individual value structures. Another is to make the components of individual value structures more internally consistent. Using Lenning's (1977a) basic definition, *attitudes* can be seen as the disposition of an individual to react either positively or negatively to something in particular—

persons or types of persons, things, or situations, which predisposes an individual to act in particular ways. Defined somewhat more broadly, *values* are strong preferences based upon what is seen as desirable, important, and worthy of esteem. Both of these elements are embodied in personal belief systems and standards of conduct that cut across different aspects of an individual's life. Development of such a value structure is held by some as the ultimate goal of the undergraduate experience—for example, the personalized value structure embodied in Chickering's notion of "integrity" (1969). For other kinds of instructional programs, however, broad attitudinal development will be seen as entirely irrelevant.

A partial list of the components of this dimension would include:

- beliefs (including religious beliefs), belief systems, value commitments, and philosophies of life
- mores, customs, and standards of conduct
- patterns of feelings and emotions, including particular satisfactions and dissatisfactions with individuals, groups, institutions, and social situations

Attitudes toward Self (Development of Identity)

For some observers, the development of individual identity represents the ultimate objective of the undergraduate experience. Partially this is a result of confining investigation to a particular type of student, the traditional 18- to 21-year-old, who may be expected to undergo transformations of personal identity simply by virtue of his or her developmental stage. In examining adult or nontraditional students, however, it may make sense to investigate the degree to which the educational experience has reinforced, threatened, or transformed existing self-concepts. Discussions of self-concept also overlap with some elements of practical competence, particularly in the areas of leadership and organizational skills. Finally, this heading seems an appropriate location for the wide range of factors covered by classic psychological personality inventories.

A list of components for this dimension might include:

- perception of self, general self-concept, self-discovery
- self-reliance, self-confidence, including adventurousness and initiative, autonomy, and independence
- satisfaction with self, psychological well-being
- personality/personal coping characteristics, including flexibility and adaptability, dogmatism/authoritarianism, tolerance and persistence, and so forth

Attitudes toward Others

Like the development of individual identity, development of appropriate attitudes toward others is probably worthy of separate treatment as an outcome dimension because of its special place as a part of the presumed "humanizing" effect of higher education. Indeed, the two are generally held to reinforce one another: a strong, well-balanced self-concept will aid the development of a tolerant, open, judicious approach to others who may have different values and characteristics.

Possible components of this dimension will undoubtedly overlap considerably with general values and belief systems. Such components might include:

- specific perceptions of other individuals/groups in society
- tolerance for cultural and intellectual diversity, including a willingness to accept different points of view
- general human understanding, including empathy, sensitivity, and cooperation

CLASSIFICATION

Relationships with Society and with Particular Constituencies

Explicit changes in the three major dimensions of outcomes—knowledge, skills, and attitudes/values—are presumed to be direct results of the educational process. Many of these changes may also be assessed directly, through testing instruments or other cognitive and psychological-measurement procedures. Many, however, will only be indirectly observable through induced changes in behavior. Most such behavior will be manifested in the relationships that individuals create or maintain with particular groups or individuals in society. Observation and documentation of such relationships thus represent an alternative approach to assessing the effects of postsecondary educational experience.

More importantly, particular constituencies in society *value* educational outcomes to the degree that they positively influence such relationships. For the employer, for example, production of particular knowledge, skill, and attitudinal outcomes is important only insofar as job performance is enhanced. Assessment of these relationships as independent dimensions is thus additionally important because it is these kinds of outcomes that will be first and most critically examined by those outside the higher-education enterprise.

At least four key relationships need to be examined, each of which deals with a student's interaction with a particular set of societal constituencies.

Relationships with Educational Institutions

A first set of relationships concerns ongoing participation in postsecondary educational experiences. Participation includes persistence within a particular curriculum or course of study, further programmatic education after graduation or certification, and involvement in adult education or lifelong learning. Different educational programs, of course, have different intents with respect to such participation. Traditional undergraduate liberal-arts programs, for example, may include an expectation that a student will be both positively oriented toward graduate education and explicitly prepared for a particular program of graduate or professional study. Community-college transfer programs contain similar expectations for continued participation beyond program completion. But many postsecondary programs will contain no such presumptions and will place no particular value upon subsequent educational participation.

A minimum set of components for this dimension would include:

- individual educational development goals, including change, stability, and intensity of such goals
- patterns of enrollment, placement, and participation
- patterns of retention, attrition, and program completion
- patterns of program/institutional change or transfer
- levels of achievement in subsequent educational experiences
- patterns of actual student behavior while enrolled (for example, quality of student effort)
- assessed relevance and contribution of past education to subsequent educational experiences

Relationships with Employers/Industries

Employers and industries represent the largest and most vocal consumers of postsecondary educational "products." Indeed, growing numbers are themselves becoming suppliers of postsecondary instruction. Different kinds of employers will, of course, value quite different kinds of educational outcomes, especially in particular skills areas. In general, however, the following kinds of components seem appropriate:

- individual employment/career-choice goals, including change, stability, and intensity of such goals
- first job obtained after education/training, including the relevance of this job to the education received
- long-term employment history by occupation and industry, including the relevance of positions held to the education received
- income/earnings history
- promotion and job performance, including the assessed contribution to job performance of the education/training received
- job satisfaction

Relationships with Professions

Many professions represent organized constituencies distinct from particular employers or industries. The primary aims of such professional constituencies are to ensure that standards of competence and skill are maintained, to certify competence and skill, and to provide for professional development opportunities for members of the profession. Examples of such organized, certifying professions include such familiar occupations as engineering, medicine, teaching, business, and social-service work. Also included under this heading are relationships with such bodies as labor unions and organized public-employee groups.

Particular aspects of this relationship that should be considered include:

- individual professional-development goals, including change, stability, and intensity of these goals
- patterns of professional certification/recognition/award
- patterns of subsequent professional-development activities
- assessed contributions of past education/training to professional success
- professional satisfaction

Peter Ewell

Relationships with Family/Community/Society

In addition to the three constituencies discussed above, many other explicit societal groups with an interest in postsecondary education could be identified. At this point, however, it seems sufficient to consider all such groups under a single heading. In many respects, this group of outcomes represents a behavioral counterpart to general attitudes and philosophy of life. Indeed, those educational programs that aim particularly at the development of individual "identities" generally make significant implicit claims about the way such value structures have an impact on social function and participation. There is a vast but unsystematic literature that treats impacts of this kind, ranging from family roles and structure to civic, social, and political participation.

Some of the explicit components of this dimension include:

- family roles, relationships, and child-rearing practices
- patterns of social affiliation, group membership, and participation
- patterns of voluntary contribution, including contributions of time, money, or other support
- patterns of citizenship activities/political participation

CHAPTER 4

Valuation of Particular Outcomes Dimensions

O utlining a particular set of outcomes dimensions for post-secondary education tells us very little about how these attributes should be valued or assessed by different constituencies. At least three types of constituencies—societal interest groups, students, and institutions—will have an interest in such valuations and assessments. And each will view accountability for excellence in a somewhat different way.

It is important once again to stress that valuation is a complex and multidimensional issue. One of the greatest misperceptions current among those in colleges and universities is that others in society view the outcomes of higher education in terms similar to the ones they use. Partly this is because higher education has exercised a historic claim on the creation of values. One of the primary attributes of the academy in its humanistic role has been to articulate value positions and to constitute a forum for examining alternative value structures, regardless of the external environment. Indeed, a traditional aim of liberal education has been to *create* values of particular kinds in students.

Peter Ewell

A single set of value orientations, however broad, is no longer a uniform objective of all higher-education institutions. Institutions exist for quite different purposes; some espouse quite dissimilar value positions and some purport to embrace no value position at all. This is one of the major difficulties in explicitly adopting the notion of value-added assessment in higher education. The term "value added" is useful in that it calls attention to the fact that education is about change, and should be assessed as such. But the term "value added" also automatically raises the question, whose values? The valuation of *particular* educational outcomes will be quite different for different types of institutions and constituents. The actual content of any given value-added assessment will, of consequence, be value laden. And such value-laden views of society, students, and institutions, as discussed below, will result in some quite distinctive views of educational outcomes.

Societal Interest Groups

Societal interest groups include employers, professional associations, government, and all other groups or constituencies with an explicit need for trained or educated individuals. Such groups appropriately view the assessment of educational quality primarily as a process of certifying the educational product. This view is appropriate because of the overriding need of these constituencies to ensure that the claimed knowledge and skills of graduating students are actually present. Indeed, a major concern of such constituencies over the past two decades has been the steady erosion of knowledge and skill levels of B.A.-level graduates.

Two trends have resulted from this concern. First, such constituencies have increased the practice of instituting their own assessment programs to ascertain the knowledge and skill levels of current and prospective employees or participants. A recent well-publicized example is the decision of the U.S. Army to no longer accept the high-school diploma as evidence of mastery of basic skills, and to implement its own internal testing program. Many professions, of course, have relied on such a practice for years, certifying prospective members of the profession as competent to practice through an explicit examination procedure. The growing number of such programs testifies to a rising concern on the part of such external constituencies that the kinds of outcomes assessments practiced by higher-education institutions are either inadequate or inappropriate.

This concern has prompted a second trend: external constituents are now themselves providing the requisite training. Many corporations, for example, now offer not only in-house training in such fields as management and basic skills development, but also specialized training in the requirements of a particular job or profession. This results partly from a perception that colleges and universities are not meeting this need effectively (Matthews and Norgaard 1984). Furthermore, there is some evidence that corporations would readily agree that general skills training be provided by local colleges and universities if they could do so more efficiently.

Different constituencies will, of course, choose different types of outcomes as important for certification. Most, however, will value outcomes within the skills area as the most critical. Most employers and professional associations will initially be interested in the skills required for effective performance within a particular well-specified job situation. In some cases, these will be highly specialized and individual skills, such as those associated with the operation of a particular piece of equipment or a technical procedure. In other cases, the distinctive element is a *combination* of skills unique to a particular job or profession. In such cases, employers and professionals may well insist that actual performance in real situations (or simulations of real situations) be assessed in order to determine competence.

Peter Ewell

Employer and professional groups are also interested in ensuring that students possess a minimum competence in verbal, quantitative, and analytic/problem-solving skills. It is in the provision of such basic skills that employers, professions, and government rely most heavily on institutions of higher education, and where their concerns about quality have been most vocal. Many related concerns center around the degree to which individuals have the capacity to learn and relearn specialized job skills in a rapidly changing environment. A number of industries are, in this regard, rediscovering the value of the traditional balanced liberal-arts curriculum in providing adaptable and flexible manpower. Indeed, some have discovered that the kinds of skills provided by a general education are often, in the long run, more valuable to productivity than those provided by more narrowly focused courses of study.

Who should have the responsibility for conducting such assessment is a difficult question. In one sense, the ultimate assessment is ongoing and behavioral: Do students obtain employment and perform effectively in job situations? If the value of postsecondary education is negligible, the marketplace will soon find it out. One option, therefore, is simply to let this process take its course. As noted above, a second option, already practiced by many professions, is to conduct independent assessments of the educational product through certification or licensure examinations. This has the significant advantage of separating the assessment process from those who provide the education—a principle that has considerable proven effectiveness from a learning standpoint. A second advantage of separation is that it allows different kinds of assessment to take place for different purposes. Many legitimate independent assessments may be simultaneously undertaken without the appearance of there being one single summative judgment of institutional or program quality.

Faced with a significant level of external concern about student competence, many institutions have begun a process of internal "product assessment" to demonstrate, in a competitive manner, the quality of their graduates. So as the credibility of such a process is maintained, this type of testing program may have significant advantages over external assessment because the detailed results of the process may be directly used in program improvement. The second part of this book will contain several examples of summative assessment programs of this kind.

Students

Students and potential students are a constituency often overlooked in discussions of quality. Yet as Pace (1983) has pointed out, students are probably the best and most appropriate judges of the educational experiences they have undergone. For different kinds of students, of course, valuation of the educational experience will proceed along quite different outcomes dimensions. Some students will seek to gain specific skills appropriate to a particular occupation or career. Others will seek general education as fulfillment of a much more general perceived need or expectation. Many others will not know what they are looking for.

Despite this variety, the systematic assessment of student goals and the comparison of student goals with student outcomes have been a strangely neglected activity in higher education. In large measure, this has been the case because educators expect student goals and aspirations to be uniform. For most institutions, in fact, degree completion is assumed to be a primary reason for attendance.

For many types of students, however, the actual completion of a program may be only a small part of an educational agenda. Much attrition occurs because students perceive that program completion at a given institution is not fulfilling their broader educational goals. Indeed, what students are actually looking for may only be discovered at many institutions when they drop out without having found it. But a great deal of attrition also occurs because broader educational goals *have* been met, and explicit program completion was not one of them.

This is a situation increasingly recognized by community colleges and other vocationally oriented institutions. Students may attend such institutions purely to master a particular employment-related skill or to attain a given level of basic-skills proficiency. Consequently, they are not interested in the many other potential benefits of completing a degree program and will withdraw from such a program when they have obtained what they were seeking. Similarly, many two-year transfer students will decide to move to a senior institution the moment they feel that they can successfully move. They do so regardless of their status in the completion of an associate degree at the institution in which they were originally enrolled. Such students—often counted as program dropouts—have actually successfully attained their own valued outcomes with respect to a particular educational institution.

As a result, many such institutions are beginning to recognize the vast disparities in the goals of enrolled students. Often this will entail systematic assessment and classification of different student "prototypes" of the kind being investigated by community colleges in California (Sheldon 1981). In other cases, it will simply entail recognition of the disparity of student goals and will temper student success and retention analyses as a result (Walleri 1981).

Traditional four-year institutions have historically been less subject to great disparities in student goals—partly because their admissions processes select students most clearly matching their own institutional environment. Even within such institutions, however, student goals, as revealed by particular behavior patterns, can come as a surprise to faculty and administrators. Astin, for example, has recently documented a broad shift in student values and aspirations as revealed through survey responses and choice of academic program (Astin 1984c). In addition, a number of institutions, after investigating patterns of student changes of major, are discovering that these are less related to subject matter than to social or career aspiration. The choice of program is based upon an anticipated income and life-style, not an inherent interest in the subject to be mastered. (Frustrated biology majors, for example, enter pre-law programs rather than pursuing another science, largely because they originally aspired to the life-style and income associated with medicine, not necessarily to a medical career.)

Assessments of educational quality, of course, should not rest solely on "consumer satisfaction." Indeed, an avowed purpose of many institutions of higher education is to *change* student perceptions and aspirations and, consequently, to shape the patterns of student valuation. And there is ample institutional evidence that such value shifts do occur in the course of a four-year liberal-arts curriculum.

But it seems equally clear that any institution that does not pay systematic attention to the match between student aspirations and actual educational outcomes is doing both its students and society a serious disservice. Students will, in fact, differ in what they wish to accomplish through higher education; we must not assume that the act of enrollment itself automatically entails a decision on the part of a given student to accept the values of a particular institution as his or her own. And these differences will have considerable impact on the ultimate outcomes.

Institutions

Institutions have the greatest responsibility for assessing and valuing educational outcomes. Different institutions will, of course, have vastly different conceptions of the types of outcomes they intend to produce. Despite these differences, all have a responsibility to articulate such outcomes, to examine their success in attaining these outcomes, and to make changes in programs and services to improve their effectiveness. Several examples of the way particular institutions have discharged this responsibility will be presented in the following chapters.

Regardless of the institutional value system imposed, there are at least two distinct ways of conducting such assessments. The first is the most straightforward—evaluation of the effectiveness or quality of a particular institution or program should consider the *absolute* increments of gain achieved on a set of identified, valued outcomes dimensions. This requires that particular valued outcomes be identified in advance and that an explicit mechanism for assessing gain be put into place. Results of assessment may then be used to identify programmatic weaknesses and make needed changes.

A second way of looking at assessment is to look not simply at absolute gains, but at *patterns* or *profiles* of development across dimensions. For many institutions, the shape of the outcomes profile—that is, which dimensions are high relative to others—is at least as important as absolute gain on any given dimension. This may be especially true of institutions with a particular values orientation based upon religion or educational philosophy. Furthermore, because precise measurement of many outcomes dimensions is impossible, evaluations of student profiles on entry and exit may be of greater ultimate value to institutions than attempts to measure absolute gain. In practice, most institutions will probably want to use both approaches; informally, in fact, many already do.

Regardless of the values placed on higher education by different segments of society, institutions have a substantial independent responsibility to implement explicit, systematic, outcomes-oriented assessment programs to improve the quality and to maintain the credibility of their educational products. And, as the examples in the chapters of part 2 will show, such explicit assessment programs are far more viable, less costly, and less disruptive than many may think.

Achieving Excellence: The Attributes of Successful Institutional- Assessment Programs

Being able to articulate educational goals effectively does not amount to achieving them. Institutional improvement will require taking a wide range of actions. Some actions will concentrate on the curriculum, some on faculty and instructional-resource development, and some on the configuration and content of the learning environment. The particular mix and substance of actions directed toward improvement will, of course, depend upon individual institutional circumstances. Each such institutional-improvement strategy will, however, be successful only to the degree that it is planned, coordinated, and evaluated in the context of good information.

The objective of part 2 of this book is to illustrate some basic design principles for gathering and using such information. These principles are based upon a growing body of institutional experience. To begin the discussion, chapter 5 provides examples of three particularly successful institutional-assessment programs. Each is located in a distinct setting, and each approaches the task of assessment in a somewhat different way. Chapter 6 discusses some of the most common objections to establishing such a program at a college or university campus—among them, faculty resistance, excessive cost, and lack of administrative incentive. Finally, chapter 7 outlines some important themes common to all successful efforts and illustrates them with examples drawn from actual institutional practice.

To anticipate, all efforts to establish institutional self-assessment and improvement programs share four basic requirements:

1. Such efforts must be founded upon attempts to articulate the specific educational goals of the institution as explicitly and as comprehensively as possible. In short, each institution should regularly and systematically address the question of how it will affect its students and along which kinds of outcomes directions it intends and expects positive changes. Most current statements of institutional mission—particularly those typical of public institutions—imply an intent to be everything to everyone. Such statements are of limited value for setting institutional direction. Moreover, considerable evidence suggests that institutions seriously attempting to implement such strategies, particularly in hard times, are ineffective as a result (Chaffee 1984). Needless to say, the process of articulating instructional goals must also be highly participatory. Greatly dependent upon faculty involvement and commitment, this process may proceed most effectively at the instructional unit or department level.

2. Such efforts must be founded upon visible, explicit, institution-specific information. Such information can be of many kinds drawn from many sources, but it must be collected systematically and organized in terms of specific outcomes categories identified in the initial phase of assessment. It is important to stress that while information of this kind should be as accurate as is feasible, standards of accuracy are less important than are standards of relevance. Most data that enter such an assessment process will be suggestive rather than determinative. Indeed, a successful data-gathering effort designed to support institutional assessment depends on its use of multiple criteria and measurement devices. There is a growing body of evidence to suggest that the explicit presence of concrete information in an assessment situation may, in itself, have as much to do with generating improvement as its empirical content or its direct implications (Braskamp 1982). In addition to informing policy, explicit data collection serves as a symbol of commitment and a focus of attention (Feldman and March 1981, Ewell and Chaffee 1984). Critical to this process are institutionwide structures that require both extensive and formal participation across units and departments in discussions of the implications of assessment data.

3. **Such efforts should be equally founded upon a set of administrative incentives to reward those in the institution who are willing to undertake information-based qualitative improvements in programs and services.** Such strategies will take many forms, but all should include mechanisms for effectively disseminating student-assessment information, for encouraging individual academic departments and support units to make changes as a result of this information, and for using ongoing assessment information to monitor the effectiveness of any changes made. Evidence that implementation of such strategies is feasible has grown considerably with completion of two national projects on the institutional use of information on student outcomes (Ewell 1984; Kemerer, Baldridge, and Green 1982), and with a number of exemplary individual institutional programs. Successful programs of this kind take substantial care to disseminate assessment information to the campus community in an accessible, nontechnical, and issue-oriented manner. On most campuses, such information, if disseminated at all, is communicated in the form of technical reports that are as daunting as they are irrelevant to the decisions that faculty and practicing administrators have to make.

A second characteristic of these exemplary efforts is that assessment information, once disseminated, is used to structure a campus dialogue. In many cases, this dialogue is formal and written, consisting of unit responses to questions about unit-specific assessment findings in the context of a formal strategic planning, budget planning, or program-review process. In other cases, the dialogue is less formal and highly participatory, consisting of faculty/staff retreats or committee discussions centered around a particular issue of student success revealed by the assessment. In both cases, a key to success has been the role of assessment information to raise questions rather than to make judgments. Like all incentive systems, those that rely upon rewarding success are more generally effective in the long term than those that rely on imposing negative sanctions for poor performance.

4. Such efforts should be designed to include appropriate participation on the part of faculty, administration, and students. The results of assessment should be used in such a manner that further discussion is encouraged and self-sustaining. The ultimate objective of institutional self-assessment programs is to encourage active discussion of educational issues, policies, and content. As in any other educational process, the intent is to focus faculty and administrative attention on evaluating, restructuring, and delivering the curriculum and institutional learning environment. In most institutions, there are at present few opportunities for promoting this kind of discussion and involvement. Most administrators are rightly concerned with day-to-day problems. Faculty members are similarly concerned with research and service activities. Such activities hardly constitute distractions. Nevertheless, most institutions offer few opportunities or forums that allow professional time to be allocated to the examination of teaching and learning.

Combining these four basic requirements for an explicit, comprehensive, information-based assessment structure is not a simple task. Furthermore, each campus must approach the task on its own terms and within the limits and opportunities provided by its own context. Certainly, successful efforts share a number of characteristics, but it is important to recognize that perhaps the most salient characteristic of successful efforts has been consistency of implementation throughout the campus. This lends an organic quality to the undertaking. All successful efforts involve, as a prerequisite, a clear understanding of educational objectives. Each campus engaged in such an effort has made a conscious choice as to which of many possible types of educational outcomes it most intends to achieve. Each, therefore, has a clear idea of what "educational excellence" means within its own particular context. And it is important to recall that many such definitions of excellence are possible and legitimate.

CHAPTER 5

Three Examples of Institutional Self-Assessment

Because of the many differences among postsecondary institutions, development of an institutional self-assessment process will be far from uniform. Different institutions have developed different processes for different purposes, depending both upon their individual structures and upon what kinds of educational outcomes they would like their students to acquire. The three brief cases presented in this chapter reflect this diversity. They also emphasize that creation of a campuswide assessment structure is an *organic* exercise, reliant as much upon the relationships among its parts as upon the particular tools, techniques, and strategies that it employs.

At a later point we will discuss some of the common elements among all such undertakings. For the moment, however, it is important to consider such assessment efforts independently. Described below are three individual examples of institutions that have used self-assessment to address particular sets of problems:

Peter Ewell

Alverno College—Assessment and Institutional Culture

Assessment at Alverno College is strongly conditioned by the institution's distinctive history and characteristics. Located in Milwaukee, Alverno is a liberal-arts women's college with 1,500 degree students and a strong orientation toward preparing women for professional careers. In 1973, Alverno adopted a new outcome-oriented curriculum structure centered around eight basic skills dimensions: communications, analysis, problem solving, values in decisionmaking, social interaction, taking responsibility for the environment, involvement in the contemporary world, and aesthetic response. These basic abilities are defined in six increasingly complex levels that are infused throughout the curriculum, which remains configured in terms of traditional academic and professional subjects. In designing and delivering particular courses, faculty are expected to select levels of the abilities to teach toward, and assess these abilities within the structure of the discipline.

With this "outcomes matrix" in place, faculty at Alverno turned their attention to how such outcomes might be systematically assessed. Their first task was descriptive: to create criteria or descriptive statements that present a picture of the ability to be assessed. Their second task was evaluative: to use a variety of assessment techniques to match individual student performances with the descriptions embedded in the criteria at each ability level. In accomplishing the latter task, Alverno explores many techniques. Among these are the use of external assessors drawn from the Milwaukee business and professional community, and the assessment of student performance in specific task or decisionmaking situations. Information derived from those assessments is used to evaluate individual student performance. Results of assessments are provided to each student and are used to help the student improve her performance.

A key element of assessment is an explicit place for such activities—an Assessment Center, which administers these assessments external to courses. Another element is the Assessment Council, a faculty body that monitors assessment across the college and provides technical assistance to faculty. In addition, the Office of Research and Evaluation, funded by the college, systematically evaluates the curriculum as a whole, researches student development and the teaching-learning process, and provides a way for faculty to investigate their questions about student outcomes. Begun with external support from the National Institute of Education (NIE) and other sources, the Office of Research and Evaluation recently completed a seven-year longitudinal study of the impact of the Alverno curriculum as a whole on students, both during and after college.

This investigation was both comprehensive and exhaustive. The office studied over 750 four-year and 60 two-year students, using intensive interviews, performance assessments, and sixteen different assessment instruments. At the same time, professionals in several fields were surveyed to determine the kinds of skills and characteristics typical of the successful practitioner. Throughout the process, primary emphasis was placed upon validation through multiple measurement. Most attributes were measured in several different ways and at different points in time, using both locally developed and commercially available assessment instruments. Examples of the latter include Learning Style Inventories by Kolb and several exercises developed by McBer and Company, the Watson-Glaser Critical Thinking Appraisal, and measures of moral, ego, and intellectual development as described by Kohlberg, Loevinger, Piaget, and Perry.

Results also help faculty determine if particular elements of the curriculum are effective in meeting previously defined educational objectives. Indeed, a number of faculty have expanded upon the central data-collection effort by engaging in local assessments of their own seminars or programs (Mentkowski and Doherty 1984, p. 157). Finally, results of the evaluations have been used to validate the curriculum as a whole. In this regard, particular attention has been paid to longitudinal studies of how students develop as they encounter the curriculum, and the persistence of general competencies after graduation. For the most part, research showed that values and skills outcomes do persist and are recognized as important by students.

A primary aspect of assessment at Alverno is that it is firmly grounded in a theory of student development. Multiple studies are undertaken not simply to obtain "triangulation" of results, but also to understand the way students *change* in the course of their enrollment. This focus on development has many important implications. Not the least of these is that both faculty and students see such a focus as recognition of their importance as individual teachers and learners. As a result, they are willing to internalize the assessment process fully.

In sum, Alverno presents us with a case of an institution uniquely committed to integrating instruction, assessment, research, and evaluation. Consequently, theirs is a process that allows both educational improvement and an opportunity to demonstrate to the outside world that education does indeed make a difference. As Mentkowski and Doherty put it, "[This model] enables faculty to measure things they really care to change, instead of measuring outcomes for which they are held accountable but that are not their own goals. . . . That puts the faculty in the position of being able to join with the administration and with the institution as a whole in explaining to the rest of society what education does" (1984, p. 160).

Northeast Missouri State University—
Linking Outcomes with Resources

In contrast to Alverno College, Northeast Missouri State University (NMSU) presents a more generally familiar picture. Located in the small town of Kirksville, NMSU is a public regional comprehensive university with a largely residential student body of approximately 7,000. Traditionally organized, NMSU offers an array of programs that most institutions of its size and type would recognize. What is less familiar is that for the past five years NMSU has engaged in a comprehensive assessment of "value added" in its student body, using readily available standardized testing instruments (McClain 1984). Furthermore, the institution has used the results of this process explicitly, both to make resource-allocation decisions on campus and to support its requests for program-improvement dollars from state funding authorities.

Assessment at NMSU involves three linked activities. The first of these consists of a value-added assessment of student gains in general education between the freshman and junior years. In order to assess value added, students are administered the ACT Assessment at the beginning of their freshman year (most, in fact, enter having taken the ACT) and again at the end of their sophomore year. More recently, half the student body has been given the ACT-COMP (College Outcome Measures Project) instrument to supplement the value-added portion of the assessment. Difference scores are calculated on the basis of freshman and sophomore performance, then reported to the academic community.

The second activity in the NMSU assessment program is a standardized test of achievement in the major field, administered at the completion of each student's program. Where applicable, all students complete the relevant GRE field examination, or a preprofessional or certification instrument where available. Scores for NMSU students are then compared with national norms, and where possible, subscores are used to evaluate particular portions of the curriculum.

The third activity in NMSU's assessment project involves surveying student opinion using several standardized attitudinal instruments administered at different points in the student's career. Student opinions are gathered by means of questionnaires for entering, continuing, and graduating students, and alumni follow-up studies. As at Alverno, students are informed about the assessment process from the beginning and are encouraged to see the process as symbolic of the institution's commitment to evaluate and improve instruction.

In contrast to Alverno, however, assessment at NMSU is a relatively low-overhead operation. Coordination of the process is centered in the office of the Dean of Instruction, and assessment data are distributed to academic division heads and student-service personnel for local interpretation and use. Because the process relies heavily upon existing standardized instruments for which computer scoring is available, it is neither expensive nor difficult to administer.

Results of the assessment process have been used at NMSU in many ways. Several individual curricula have been strengthened as a result of senior achievement test results. Score gains on the value-added assessment have pointed to the need to increase writing requirements across the curriculum. In a number of cases, changes in the curriculum have resulted in marked improvement in the competitive performances of NMSU students on national normed achievement tests. Most strikingly, results of the assessment process have substantiated NMSU's appropriations requests for the past three years. Requests for additional state dollars have been explicitly linked with proposed improvements in student performance in identified areas; appropriate targets for such improvements have been identified for several future years. This approach to funding represents a radical departure from the traditional enrollment-driven model, and it is one that many public institutions are carefully watching.

Compared to the Alverno model, assessment at NMSU is a limited activity. Rather than developing an assessment process from the ground up, NMSU has chosen instead to commit limited resources in an attempt to match existing assessment instruments with a more traditional set of program offerings. While the scope of the effort has been limited, the impact on the campus has been considerable. As at Alverno, the largest impact has been the way in which the assessment process has focused faculty and administrative attention on student learning and development. And as at Alverno, this attention has many implications for the credibility of the educational product. As President McClain (1983, p. 6) writes in a description of assessment at NMSU, "The model NMSU has implemented is one that can be used by any institution of higher education. . . . Through the use of this value-added system of assessment, the University aims to maximize its human and technological resources for the education of its students. It aims to be sure it is providing quality education which assures its students of competency in the marketplace upon graduation."

The University of Tennessee, Knoxville—
Performance Funding and Institutional Response

As a large, complex public research institution, the University of Tennessee, Knoxville (UTK) requires an institutional assessment vastly different from those of Alverno College and Northeast Missouri State University (NMSU). Although teaching is a strong priority at UTK, it is by no means the sole focus of institutional activity. Nor can it be said that UTK has a single campus culture or identity. Like most large research institutions, UTK consists of many such cultures existing simultaneously in the university's schools and departments.

The roots of assessment at UTK lie in a unique approach to budgeting in statewide public higher education. In 1979, the Tennessee Higher Education Commission (THEC) initiated a program termed "performance funding," setting aside a designated percentage of the state's annual higher-education budget (initially 2 percent, now 5 percent of the total educational and general budget) for distribution to individual institutions on the basis of identified criteria for institutional performance (Bogue and Brown 1982). Currently, funds are awarded according to five such criteria: (1) the percentage of programs eligible for accreditation at the institutions that are accredited, (2) student achievement in general education (value-added), (3) student performance in the major field, (4) student satisfaction with the educational experience, and (5) the existence of an established plan for using the results of assessment to improve educational programs. The incentives for assessment provided to institutions by this program are considerable. Much, however, depends upon how each campus elects to respond.

For UTK, an opportunity for helping develop a response came with the institution's participation in the NCHEMS/Kellogg Student Outcomes Project, a three-year, multi-institutional effort to demonstrate the use of student-outcomes information in program planning and decisionmaking (Banta 1984). The project provided UTK with a limited amount of funding to develop campuswide assessments of learning outcomes consistent with the THEC criteria. To begin the project on campus, three task forces composed of faculty and administrators conducted extensive reviews of assessment methodologies in general education, achievement in the major field, and student satisfaction. Recommendations of these task forces—transmitted to the chancellor and to chief academic administrators in each of the university's sixteen colleges and schools—served as the basis for constructing a comprehensive assessment process for the university.

As at NMSU, a first component of this assessment process involves administering the ACT-COMP examination to freshmen and to seniors to assess the "value added" of the collegiate experience in general education. By analyzing relationships between COMP subscores and many other factors (for example, patterns of student course work), the university has a good basis for identifying elements of the curriculum that contribute most to general education. Results of this analysis are used by a campuswide coordinating committee on general education and by counterpart committees in each college as they review and revise particular curricula.

THREE EXAMPLES

A second component of the UTK assessment effort involved initiating pilot projects in fourteen departments to experiment with new methods of measuring outcomes in the major field. Seven departments used standardized tests or locally developed instruments to measure cognitive learning gains; seven others surveyed currently enrolled students, program graduates, or employers of program graduates to assemble evaluative data. As at Alverno and NMSU, the process of selecting or designing a comprehensive examination in the discipline was particularly important in bringing department faculty together explicitly to consider curriculum goals and objectives. The success of these pilot efforts has resulted in a directive from the provost's office that comprehensive testing of graduates be considered by the faculty of each of the university's 109 degree programs.

A third component of the assessment project at UTK involved faculty-designed instruments for assessing student and graduate satisfaction. The instruments and methodologies for these assessments were designed by UTK faculty in sociology and political science, with considerable consultation with the campus community. Therefore, administrators, department heads, and faculty were given a vested interest in the results. In several instances, the general university survey has prompted an interest at the department level in conducting more detailed follow-up inquiries.

Because of the size and complexity of UTK, central direction of learning assessment has been critical. A key aspect of the assessment effort is the role of the project coordinator—a full-time faculty member in educational measurement and psychology, whose office is in the university's Learning Research Center. In addition to assembling and documenting the results of various assessment studies, the coordinator also serves as a technical consultant to schools and departments wishing to construct and administer their own assessments. A particularly important responsibility of the coordinator is the construction of individual college or department reports that succinctly summarize results, by unit, in all three areas of assessment (general education, achievement in the major field, and student satisfaction). These reports are followed up with in-person consultation between the coordinator and the unit head (often including selected or interested members of the unit's faculty) to develop the specific implications of assessment information. These consultations have resulted in numerous changes in departmental policies, curricula, and organization.

In contrast to Alverno and NMSU, assessment at UTK has been both more decentralized and more reactive. As a large, complex research institution with a strong departmental structure, UTK's assessment appropriately places considerable responsibility upon individual academic units. Individual units have been given a great deal of latitude in developing and using their own assessment instruments and procedures. And indeed, those designing their own procedures, rather than simply adopting existing measures, also have been the most successful in using the results. But the role of central administration in providing incentives and resources to undertake assessment has been equally important. The use of outcomes information in the university's program-review and budgeting processes, as well as the willingness of central administration to support the technical assistance role of the project coordinator, has been particularly important in securing a high level of departmental response to assessment.

Not least important to the success of assessment at UTK, of course, has been the THEC performance-funding initiative. Without the external financial incentives provided by performance funding, it is probable that an assessment project of this type and magnitude could never have been undertaken at a large public research university. Furthermore, had the institution chosen to respond defensively rather than creatively to the challenge of performance funding, such results would have been equally impossible. In sum, the UTK case is a superb example of how external agencies and central administrations can work together to create a structure of incentives and opportunities for individual departmental faculties to examine critically and, subsequently, to improve curriculum and instructional practice.

Each of these three institutions has approached the task of assessment in its own way, consistent with its unique goals, its particular institutional philosophy, and its available resources. All, however, have designed and implemented programs based on explicit information about educational outcomes. These programs then use such information in concrete ways to stimulate program improvement. In building their programs, all have also had to find answers to many objections—internal and external— to establishing measurement-based assessment mechanisms. Some of the most common such objections, and the ways they can be met, are considered in the following chapter.

CHAPTER 6

Some Common Objections to Institutional Self-Assessment

T he three cases discussed in the previous chapter are in many respects atypical of most higher-education institutions, both in the extent and the quality of their self-assessment efforts. As such, it is easy to dismiss them as "outliers" in the more general distribution of institutional types. Alverno is a women's college with an explicitly nontraditional curriculum. Its self-assessment efforts have been particularly bound up both with the availability of external funds to support the effort and with the uniquely innovative qualities and commitments of the institution's basic identity. Northeast Missouri State University (NMSU) is, in many ways, quite traditional. But it possesses an institutional leadership unusually committed to self-assessment. NMSU is also character- ized by an administratively lean management style, which fosters a good deal of initiative and innovation at the unit level. The University of Tennessee, Knoxville (UTK) has experienced the mixed advantages of being the major research institution in the first state to experiment with funding higher education on perfor- mance rather than enrollment. It could well be argued by those reluctant to undertake such programs that institutions such as these are, for various reasons, special cases and that their experiences are consequently of little relevance to most postsecondary institutions.

Indeed, the common response to most innovations in higher education is, "That's all very well, but it won't work here." The vast majority of objections, however, tend to fall into one of three basic categories. Some illustrations of how each type has commonly been met are certainly in order.

Objections Based on Faculty Resistance

Many of the most vehement objections to the systematic assessment of institutional impact will come from faculty. Generally, these objections are of two quite different kinds, although the rhetoric of objection will often combine the two. A first reason for resistance is a fear on the part of faculty that they will be negatively evaluated. A second basis is more philosophical: a conviction that the outcomes of what they do in the classroom are inherently unmeasurable by anyone but the faculty.

Turning to the first source of resistance, faculty often confuse assessments of program effectiveness with course evaluation—a process that, on many campuses, is notoriously inaccurate or biased. In many cases, these two quite different processes have not been well distinguished. A key element in securing faculty cooperation from the outset, therefore, is to ensure that the focus of assessment is placed quite clearly on the *curriculum*, and that faculty are themselves fully involved in the process of designing key aspects of the assessment.

One of the most important aspects of the assessment process at UTK, for example, is its focus on curriculum in the individual department. In the political science and geography departments, patterns of student-assessment information led faculty to question the effectiveness of the department's introductory course. In both cases, the introductory course was shown to be too unfocused and in need of redirection. Subsequently, an effort was undertaken to improve these courses. In one of these departments the investigation did involve looking at the relationship between individual instructors and assessment results. However, these data were handled extremely carefully by the department chair. Course-specific results became the basis of conversations between the chair and individual faculty members, but these conversations were not included as part of a formal performance evaluation.

Faculty resistance based upon fear of negative evaluation is often heavily bound up with more basic objections to measurement of any kind. Many faculty are simply philosophically opposed to explicit outcomes measurement. They feel that it is inherently misleading, oversimplifying, or inaccurate. Moreover, many faculty believe that assessments designed to tap general attributes do not adequately reflect the specific emphases that they feel are present in their classrooms.

Two ways of meeting these objections are well illustrated by the three cases presented earlier. The first approach is to recognize publicly the inadequacy of any *single* outcome measure or indicator and to collect as many measures of program effectiveness as possible. This theme is strongly apparent both in Alverno's triangulated approach, in UTK's construction of department and school profiles that merge the results of many data-collection efforts, and in NMSU's use of information on both cognitive performance and student satisfaction.

The efficacy of this approach may be illustrated by many other institutional examples. When the State University of New York at Albany (SUNY-Albany) distributed department-specific results of an alumni survey as part of the institution's annual planning/budgeting cycle, both quantitative and verbal responses were provided. Interviews with department heads later indicated that the presence of both kinds of information built much greater confidence in the accuracy of assessment information. At North Carolina State University (NCSU), the assessment process brought together data on black student recruitment, retention, academic achievement, campus perceptions, and student behavior. Individual pieces of information, previously seen as substantially without implications, when interpreted and integrated revealed a striking picture of the patterns of minority-student success and failure.

A second basic method of overcoming faculty resistance is to involve faculty directly in the design of the assessment process. Faculty involvement is strongly apparent in the case material presented earlier. Alverno's assessment process is explicitly based upon the curricular dimensions of competency previously developed by the institution's faculty. And at UTK, assessments of general education were substantially aided by a series of faculty seminars on the ACT-COMP examination, the basis for data collection on general education. The positive tone set by these seminars was particularly important to the project's success. Seminar leaders were careful to point out the many limits of the particular measurement approach used and to enlist faculty interest in making careful, creative, nonjudgmental use of the results.

Other examples stress the importance of involving faculty in the interpretation of assessment results. Spoon River College (SRC), a small rural community college, made student-assessment results the centerpiece of annual day-long faculty in-service retreat days. Explicit findings about student abilities, enrollment behavior, perceptions of the institution, and postgraduate place-ment were used to structure discussions of how to better retain particular populations of students. Similarly, both Mount Hood Community College (MHCC) and Towson State University (TSU) have effectively used campuswide student-success com-mittees to systematically review the implications of institutional-assessment information. In all such cases, broad participation has produced better and more sensitive insights into the implications of particular assessment results. More importantly, involvement has had a positive impact on the attitudes of many faculty toward instructional issues. Many now report that, as a result of the information provided, they are more sensitive to student concerns and more prone to question previously unexamined elements of the curriculum.

In short, the primary method for overcoming faculty resistance to explicit institutional assessment is to make faculty full partners in the process from the outset. It is, after all, in individual classrooms that assessment information will be either used or forgotten.

Objections Based on Excessive Cost

Many objections to establishing a comprehensive program of institutional-assessment center on the costs associated with doing so. The primary argument is that useful, accurate information on student achievement and instructional effectiveness is not currently available on most campuses and that providing such information entails establishment of an expensive data-collection "superstructure" largely divorced from academic affairs. Most faculty and many administrators are understandably reluctant to support the diversion of considerable resources from the main business of teaching and doing research.

Admittedly, assessment efforts such as Alverno's can be expensive and require a careful look at institutional priorities. Alverno's budgetary commitment to assessment is backed by a faculty committed to assessing student learning as a developmental process, as well as to the more traditional program-evaluation goal of assessment. And, clearly, institutions should attempt efforts of such magnitude and direction only when there is a strong collective mandate to do so. For NMSU and UTK, the issue of resource investment is a good deal less clear-cut. NMSU, for example, maintains its comprehensive assessment program with the investment of relatively few additional institutional resources. The use of commonly available assessment instruments such as the ACT Assessment, the ACT-COMP, and standardized student surveys have made the data-collection effort at NMSU unusually efficient. At UTK, moreover, the primary expense has been in providing administrative coordination for the assessment project—particularly in the provision of technical assistance to departments and schools wishing to design their own instruments to assess student progress in the major field.

In many cases, development of an initial institutional-assessment process involves minimal additional expense because institutions already collect a great deal of information about students. Indeed, one part of Alverno's triangulated model concentrates on data already collected. One major intent of the recently completed NCHEMS/Kellogg Student Outcomes Project was to enable institutions to make more effective use of *existing* information about student outcomes. In seven public institutions, this initial assumption of the project was strongly confirmed (Ewell 1984).

Scattered student-assessment data, however, is rarely in a form that makes it immediately useful. Different kinds of data are collected by different offices for different purposes. It is often a matter of considerable effort both to inventory the data available on a large and complex university campus and to coordinate future data-collection efforts more effectively. Institutions that have undertaken these processes, however, have generally found the exercise to be of value. At MHCC, for example, campuswide assessment included placement testing, student follow-up surveys, and assessments of the effectiveness of developmental-education programs. Each of these data-collection efforts had been previously developed by a different campus unit, but their collective implications for student success had not previously been considered. At NCSU, a similar pattern emerged. Data on black student behavior was already routinely being collected by many different academic and student-affairs offices; integrating the findings of these multiple existing efforts involved minimal additional expenditure.

OBJECTIONS TO SELF-ASSESSMENT

Such uncoordinated student assessment already consumes many institutional resources. As Astin points out (1984a), the majority of colleges and universities routinely collect information on student aptitudes and achievements to screen and place students. But the fact that different instruments are used at different times generally precludes measurement of student change over time. Some of the most effective institutional assessments make considerable use of this built-in pretest. NMSU's value-added approach, for example, relies upon the assumptions that many students will already have taken the ACT Assessment and that many students bound for graduate school will already want to take the GRE and professional aptitude or certification tests as the GMAT, LSAT, or NCTE. At UTK, moreover, approximately two-thirds of the departments that assessed achievement in the major field could also make use of existing standardized test instruments. And at Alverno, student performance at a given ability level is a built-in pretest for the next.

In short, developing a campuswide assessment process is certainly not a costless activity. Many of the examples cited have relied upon some degree of external funding to accomplish their goals (or, in the case of UTK, external incentives in the form of performance funding). In the majority of cases, however, the expenditure has been relatively modest. The average institutional investment in the NCHEMS/Kellogg project over a three-year period was approximately $35,000, matched by approximately $21,000 in external funds and services. From a marginal point of view, few equivalent investments could have yielded a higher return.

Objections Based on Lack of Administrative Incentive

Finally, there is the objection that most colleges and universities are simply not structured to take advantage of comprehensive assessment information. In most institutions, traditional academic organization is decentralized, if not fragmented. Responsibility for overall student success and development is scattered throughout many offices among many individuals, each of whom deals with a particular "piece" of the individual student. More importantly, institutional reward structures, particularly in the public sector, are centered more around productivity than around effectiveness. These two structural facts about most colleges and universities constitute a formidable challenge to information-based qualitative improvement. If the fundamental incentive structure of the institution cannot be modified to reward innovation and achievement as revealed by assessment information, then comprehensive data collection will indeed become what its critics fear—an administrative superstructure.

In the case of Alverno, this outcome was avoided by a complete remaking of the institution's curriculum. Together with the new curriculum came a new way of looking at institutional success and failure—one shared by faculty and administration alike. Few institutions will want or be in a position to undertake so radical a transformation. Many examples of less radical approaches are available, however. Some of these rely upon providing successful units with modest additional resources. Others rely upon building assessment information into a formal structure of subunit review and accountability. Finally, an increasing number are being imposed on institutions from without—by state boards, accrediting agencies, and government bodies.

Certainly, providing departments and units with direct incentives to increase performance or to collect and use additional assessment information is a promising approach. Indeed, from a state perspective, this approach constitutes the original rationale of the Tennessee Higher Education Commission's experiment in performance funding. This approach has also been effectively implemented at the campus level. The UTK assessment project, for example, provided limited "mini-grants" to departments and schools willing to undertake pilot projects in assessing student achievement in the major field. Montana State University (MSU) makes extensive use of such mini-grants, both in providing limited funds to collect and use information on student attitudes and achievements and in funding projects designed to improve faculty vitality. In most cases, the funds provided have been relatively modest and the primary effect has been to provide a visible symbol through which to recognize outstanding or innovative effort. Although symbolic, such recognition has been considerably sought after.

A more common approach has been an attempt to build student-assessment information directly into the institution's formal accountability structure. For example, at SUNY-Albany, information on student placement in jobs and in graduate schools, and student ratings of the effectiveness of departmental instruction in their major, are distributed to each department as part of the annual planning/budgeting process. Departments and schools are asked to address this information formally in the course of preparing their five-year plans and budgets. While this procedure, now two years old, has not produced notable changes in existing patterns of resource allocation, it has often significantly altered campus perceptions of what top administration feels is important. Several department heads at SUNY-Albany, for example, have structured department meetings in response to this information; this has resulted in curriculum changes.

In many cases, the focus of such efforts has been increasingly formalized in a process of academic program review. At four of the seven institutions participating in the NCHEMS/Kellogg Student Outcomes Project, for example, academic program-review processes were instituted or substantially modified. In each of these cases, information on student attitudes and achievement by department was collected and reviewed, and explicit recommendations for improvement were sought. Like the SUNY-Albany experience, these program reviews rarely produced major shifts in institutional activity. Very rarely was a program substantially modified or eliminated. However, a prime virtue of the process, reported by both faculty and administrators, was that it stimulated increased attention toward the curriculum and toward student learning.

A common theme in all of these efforts is the creation of a concrete set of incentives—both material and moral—to prompt teaching faculty and department administrators to respond explicitly to assessment information. And indeed, in many cases department chairs have reported that explicit assessment data allows them to take action on what had previously been mere suspicion. At SUNY-Albany, for example, the chair of the English department was able to use student data as authority to tighten standards in the curriculum—an action previously tabled for lack of evidence.

Such incentives are simultaneously more powerful and more threatening when implemented from outside the individual institution. Growing numbers of funding and accountability bodies, particularly in the public sector, are developing outcomes standards to apply to institutions under their jurisdiction. Certainly, the most highly developed of such programs is the performance-funding initiative in Tennessee. Unique in many ways, this program is probably most unusual in that it provides positive rewards for institutional performance. Such rewards, amounting to substantial resources in the case of major institutions, have proven to be powerful levers for the development of exemplary institutional-assessment programs such as that at UTK.

Few developing external incentive structures, however, have been so positive. More typical has been the approach of Florida in mandating specified levels of student achievement for enrollment in the upper division. Questions about student achievement and other outcome measures have increasingly been asked of public institutions in the course of state-level legislative or executive audits. While such procedures undoubtedly provide incentives for institutional improvement, they also contain the potential for considerable misuse.

OBJECTIONS TO SELF-ASSESSMENT

The external pressures generated by such state-level programs as in Tennessee or Florida have their best results in the leverage that they provide institutional administrators who want to build a case for assessment on their own campuses. This leverage has been admirably exploited, for example, in the development of department-level assessment processes at UTK in Tennessee and in the development of an academic program-review process at St. Petersburg Junior College in Florida.

It is important to stress, however, that proof of the effectiveness of such externally mandated standards ultimately lies in the *climate* these standards create for institutional self-examination. If external standards are too heavily imposed, institutions will be driven into a defensive posture. By its very nature, such a posture reverses the intended incentives. Response to external pressure becomes protective and bureaucratic—and information gathering becomes an activity that faculty either eschew or treat with cynicism. The inevitable result will be minimal impact on the classroom or curriculum.

Perhaps the most effective role of external incentives is to induce institutions to undertake certain *processes* rather than demanding a particular level of performance. The outcomes criterion for institutional accreditation currently under review by the Southern Association of Colleges and Schools provides an example of such an incentive. The essence of the criterion is that institutions should give proof that they engage in significant, information-based assessment of the outcomes they produce. There is no requirement for use of a *particular* set of outcomes dimensions or measurement procedures. Such questions are quite properly left within the prerogative of the individual institution. All that is required is that the institution take self-assessment seriously and communicate the results. The three objections to outcomes-based assessment described above constitute a formidable collective obstacle to developing systematic procedures for institutional self-examination. But they can be overcome. Perhaps the most important lesson of efforts such as the NCHEMS/

Peter Ewell

Kellogg project is the value of making a beginning. Indeed, it may be that the greatest payoffs of an institutional-assessment process lie in its initial stages, when the actual informational basis of the assessment is at its weakest. The significance of the process lies not in the facts it uncovers but in the questions it raises and in the resulting dialogue it provokes. In many of our institutions, such a dialogue will, in itself, be an accomplishment of quality.

CHAPTER 7

Four Common Themes Of "Information for Excellence" Programs

As emphasized throughout this book, every successful institutional self-assessment process must reflect the particular culture and character of the campus on which it is located. There is consequently no single recipe for success in a venture of this kind. Nevertheless, there are several themes apparent in such efforts, and those who seek to implement such programs at particular institutions are well advised to examine them.

A Focus on the Curriculum

The first major theme of successful self-assessment efforts is an explicit linkage with the institution's curriculum. Findings of the assessment must be directly relevant to current curricular issues and disseminated in such a manner that those responsible for curriculum review and development can immediately use the results. Often this will mean that the administrative center of the assessment resides in the office of the institution's chief academic-affairs officer. This is the case at Northeast Missouri State University (NSMU). At Alverno and the University of Tennessee, Knoxville (UTK), the special units charged with the responsibility for assessment have strong linkages with the formal structure of academic affairs. The efficacy of a curriculum focus has been strikingly confirmed by institutional experience in the NCHEMS/Kellogg Student Outcomes Project. At NCSU, for example, the impact of the assessment project was at first quite limited because the project was centered in a student-affairs office. Despite the comprehensiveness and quality of the data collected, few major changes were accomplished in the first two years of the project because the academic accountability structure of the institution was not directly involved. At the State University of New York-Albany (SUNY-Albany), Montana State University (MSU), and Mount Hood Community College (MHCC), moreover, the assessment effort was based in administrative offices of institutional research. While such offices brought considerable technical expertise to the assessment process, much of the challenge in these projects was to build regular relationships with deans and department chairs, those responsible for shaping and evaluating the curriculum. Success in these three campus projects was largely a product of how well these relationships were established and maintained.

These projects provide excellent illustrations of how explicit linkages can be built between those responsible for curriculum, and the information professionals who will likely be involved in any assessment project. As mentioned, regular department-specific data reports were supplied by the assessment or institutional-research office to academic administrators at SUNY-Albany, UTK, and MHCC. On each campus, the implications of the assessment data prompted departments to undertake modifications in curriculum at the department level. Often, however, the interpretive role of the information professional proved critical in making administrators aware of the limits and the potential of particular pieces of information. Indeed, one of the most important impacts of regular formal communication between data providers and data users was to create an incentive and an opportunity for a much more important pattern of ongoing informal contact.

Examples of the kinds of curriculum impacts that have been accomplished on these campuses are many. Some concern the way certain types of general or discipline-specific skills are taught and maintained. At NMSU, for example, assessment has considerably increased the number of required writing and mathematical exercises students encounter in the curriculum— and value-added assessment results have shown gains in mathematical ability as a result. At SUNY-Albany, the English department undertook similar revisions of curriculum content after receiving information that their graduates, now in graduate programs or the workplace, wished that the faculty had been "harder on them when they were enrolled."

Other examples of curriculum impact have to do with the role of particular courses in the curriculum—particularly the introductory course in a given department, or key "bottleneck" courses in a particular program that all students must pass. At North Carolina State University (NCSU), for instance, assessment revealed that a major reason why black students were not successful in many technical programs was that they were enrolling in certain courses too early. In an attempt to move through the curriculum at a faster rate, they enrolled in difficult courses before they had fully mastered important prerequisite skills. This discovery resulted in a more structured approach to the way students were advised and placed. Moreover, in a real estate program at MHCC, the order in which practice and theory courses were taught was reversed. Assessment data on the kinds of jobs students were getting after they left the program indicated a change; a shorter certification program was the result.

Peter Ewell

Many additional examples of curriculum impacts could be cited. But there are equally numerous cases where curriculum was not touched by an assessment process. The vast majority of these occurred at institutions where data collection was both physically and administratively distant from those responsible for curriculum development and where top administrators have created few incentives for the two to get together.

Choosing the Correct Unit of Analysis

A second theme of successful assessment programs follows directly from a focus on the curriculum. This theme emphasizes the importance of choosing the correct level, or unit of analysis, for campus assessment. Different institutions—depending upon their size, structure, mission, and student composition—can have vastly different patterns of human interaction. Such patterns, furthermore, are reinforced by curricular structures that encourage or discourage common course taking by students in different programs. At some institutions—particularly small, residential institutions—the entire campus may constitute the appropriate unit for assessment. At other institutions, most learning and interaction may be concentrated at the level of the department, school, or program. And at still other campuses—particularly those such as community colleges with multiple constituencies—the most appropriate units of analysis may be the several particular and distinctive types of students inhabiting the institution.

Often, of course, a single program will simultaneously approach assessment on multiple levels. At UTK and NMSU, for example, general-education assessment is reported at the campus level, while each department undertakes its own, department-specific assessment process. At SUNY-Albany, results of student follow-up surveys were used to produce campuswide issue reports on such topics as student-faculty contact and student career orientation. The same data were also broken down by depart-ment to generate local discussions of their implications. Alverno College undertook specific assessments of particular professional programs to supplement their primary assessment focus on the institution as a whole.

It is important to note that the success of these mixed strategies was strongly dependent upon the match between assess-ment and institutional culture. At Alverno, where a collective, integrated campus culture is present, campus-level results were effectively internalized and used. At SUNY-Albany and UTK, in contrast, the impact of campus-level assessments was extremely limited; results were more apparent when assessment concen-trated on individual departments. In such large, decentralized institutions, department chairs could often quite rightly claim that the results of campuswide assessments, however true, did not apply to *their* students.

This general point regarding applicability is equally telling in assessments of particular student groups. On multiconstituency campuses, it is important not to conduct assessment as though all students were alike. At Mount Hood Community College (MHCC), Spoon River College (SRC), and Towson State Univer-sity (TSU), for example, much of the assessment process consisted of developing profiles of different student "prototypes" based upon different demographic characteristics and patterns of behavior (Sheldon and Grafton 1982). At SRC, for example, five distinct types of students were identified. Each type was made the target of a different set of advisement, skills-building, and reten-tion strategies. Furthermore, all subsequent assessment reporting included distinct breakdowns and analyses for each of these five basic student populations.

The most meaningful assessment takes place at the level where students actually live and learn, where actual campus interaction takes place. One of the most interesting elements of the assessment process at MHCC, for example, is a computer-generated course report received by each faculty member for each course each term. This report contains standard enrollment information (such as major and level) on each student, but also presents data on student intentions, previous GPA, skill levels, previous education, and many other elements. The result is that faculty, particularly in large diverse classes, are much better acquainted with the needs and characteristics of the students they are facing.

The Importance of Comparison

Regardless of the unit of analysis chosen, effective comparison among units of like type should be the analytical focus of any assessment. Many types of comparison, of course, are possible, and the choice of which to use is largely a matter of institutional goals and characteristics. Comparisons of performance at the same institution over time are particularly valuable in situations where institutional goals are seen as unique and, consequently, difficult to compare to other institutions. Peer comparisons, however, are particularly valuable in assessing or demonstrating a particular institution's competitive strengths and weaknesses.

The institutions observed here have used many types of comparisons. At Alverno, specific identified abilities are a central focus of the learning environment and may not be shared by all institutions. Nevertheless, the choice of which assessment instruments to use was influenced by the availability of life-span developmental norms from other institutions. At NMSU, comparisons over time are used to chart institutional progress in value added, but departments are also evaluated in terms of their students' performances against national norms on standardized achievement tests. At SUNY-Albany and UTK, comparisons among departments are made on a number of standard indicators of student satisfaction and placement, while the same data are also analyzed campuswide by student type. In all cases, the richness and range of comparison has considerably enhanced the utility of assessment data to stimulate action.

Part of the value of a comparative orientation is that it allows effective use of data that are much "softer" than those to which administrators are often accustomed. Much of the data available on student outcomes is—as critics are quick to point out—methodologically limited. Questionnaire or test data may be biased in unknown ways due to the wording of particular questions, the characteristics of the sample, or any number of other factors. Hence, *profiles* of results are much more useful than single assessment indicators, and such profiles are most effectively presented comparatively. To know that 76 percent of the student body in a given institution is dissatisfied with advising, in itself, tells you little. However, knowing that 45 percent of the same sample last year gave the same response, or that the respective figures for English and for business students are 89 percent and 57 percent may tell you a great deal.

The most useful single set of comparisons are those that can be made among the individual academic units or programs within an institution. In the NCHEMS/Kellogg Project, mechanisms for comparing departmental performance on student outcomes—whether freestanding or as a part of an academic program-review process—were uniformly effective in generating dialogue about departmental curricula and instruction.

In their initial stages, it is important to note, not all such dialogues were cordial. Department heads and faculty were quick to point out the deficiencies of any comparisons on which they came up short. Still, all sides realized the value of a process that could inspire a dialogue on program effectiveness—a dialogue that otherwise would never have taken place. Over several years, department chairs in all participating institutions began to recognize the opportunities that the process provided for highlighting and communicating their own needs and stories.

Peter Ewell

The Importance of Involvement

All three of the above themes are subsumed in a fourth: the importance of broad participation in the construction and operation of an information-based assessment process. Promoting faculty involvement, by whatever means are at hand, is an important tactic in establishing a campuswide institutional-assessment structure. But we must not forget that faculty involvement is also the primary *end* of such a structure. Indeed, explicit institutional-assessment information is of ultimate utility only insofar as it induces faculty and administrators to regularly revisit and discuss basic educational issues.

As Astin has effectively argued, a theory of student involvement provides a comprehensive framework for organizing many discrete findings about why students learn and persist in college (Astin 1984b). According to Astin's account, it is the *sum total* of involvement in the educational process that is important, not its particular source or mix for an individual student. Some students will seek a purely academic engagement in college life and will succeed on this basis. Others will increase their "time on task" with extracurricular activities, such as work-study assignments, organized student activities, or informal contacts with others in the college environment. A primary implication of the theory is its focus on student time as a resource. Learning will be enhanced to the degree students can become (or can be induced to become) more conscious both of the ways they spend their time and the consequences of particular time investments.

If this view of effective learning is true for our students, we should explore its implications for ourselves. As teachers and administrators, we too must seriously examine our "time on task" in the business of promoting learning. One major virtue of an explicit institutional-assessment process, like the explicit curricular structures we construct for our students, is that it channels our attention toward matters we might otherwise be inclined to forget.

FOUR PROGRAM THEMES

The experiences of many colleges and universities highlight this contention. Common to all institutions participating in the NCHEMS/Kellogg project was the role of explicit assessment information in making possible discussions of institutional mission and effectiveness in the first place. Indeed, in some institutions, this general outcome was seen as having greater lasting value than any particular implications of a given data-collection effort.

At UTK, for example, some of the most important department-level impacts of assessment were in those departments that developed their *own* assessment instruments. The absence of a proven standard test of achievement in the major field was first seen as a major weakness. And in fact, the assessment instruments designed by faculty to fill the gap were admittedly crude compared to the standardized examinations available to other fields. However, the process of developing such instruments, regardless of their elegance, induced faculty to re-examine curricular objectives and methods. And the actions resulting in such departments often proved a good deal more comprehensive than in those receiving assessment information from an external source.

A similar dynamic was also apparent in general-education assessment at SUNY-Albany. To implement a new requirement for distribution-based general education, a faculty committee spent considerable effort in defining and operationalizing six dimensions of general education. While in the last analysis these dimensions differed little from those developed at many other institutions, the processes of articulating them and trying to decide how to assess them were of considerable independent value.

The use of campuswide committees to foster such discussion is one element of involvement relatively easy to accomplish. An important requirement for institutional participation in the NCHEMS/Kellogg project was that institutions constitute a broad-based committee to interpret available student-assessment information and develop recommendations as a result. The contribution of such committees to the ultimate success of the project cannot be overstated. At NCSU, for example, committee discussions immediately revealed areas where particular academic and student-service units were working at cross-purposes, or where units were unnecessarily duplicative in collecting information about students.

The effectiveness of such committees, however, depended upon more than simply creating the opportunity for people from different parts of the institution to talk about students. The fundamental difference between committee discussions within the context of the assessment project and previous institutional experience was that discussions in the context of assessment were focused and were based upon explicit information. The presence of concrete, empirical assessment data repeatedly allowed previously open and circular discussions to come to a conclusion. Interestingly, this was even the case when the assessment data provided were of limited quality. At TSU, for example, it took over a year to produce program retention data of acceptable quality, but committee discussions around preliminary data remained refreshingly concrete. Not only were actions taken as a result, but the better data available later in the assessment process revealed these to have been the proper actions.

In short, comprehensive institutional assessment provides one important structure to promote the kind of involvement in learning issues that we are likely to forget in the fragmented, means-oriented world of most higher-education institutions. Perhaps the most eloquent statement of this result comes from a faculty member at UTK: "Thanks for giving us the opportunity for doing something that we have wanted to do for a long time."

Institutional Assessment and Self-Renewal: A Developmental Metaphor

T he recently released report of the Study Group on the Conditions of Excellence in American Higher Education, sponsored by the National Institute of Education, emphasizes the need for explicit feedback and assessment to effect needed improvements in undergraduate instruction (NIE 1984). This need is based, in part, upon what we know about the effectiveness of active involvement in the learning process. Students learn better when they are actively engaged, when they are challenged, and when they are continually made aware of both the process and prospect of their own development. Administrators, teachers, and ultimately institutions themselves are no different. Improvements will result only when expectations are clear and when performance relative to these expectations is systematically assessed.

At the same time, the Study Group suggests, the landscape of higher education has changed dramatically. Institutions have grown in size, complexity, and mission. New clienteles with new needs, resources, and learning styles have been added to the traditional 18- to 21-year-old undergraduate student population. New programs and curricula, often occupationally or professionally oriented, have supplanted the traditional liberal arts as study areas of choice among undergraduate students. And, finally, these programs and curricula are increasingly delivered in new ways, often involving new technologies. Admittedly, through high selectivity, substantial resources, and a commitment to undergraduate teaching and learning, many individual colleges and universities have remained substantially unaffected by these massive environmental changes. But the majority of our institutions *have* experienced such changes—and have become larger, more diversified, and more formally structured as a result. In the face of such changes, what is to be done to revitalize undergraduate education? The answer, in part, depends upon our view of this transformation itself—whether we view these changes as reversible or inevitable, and as creative or destructive.

One of the great conceptual debates of sociology took place at the end of the nineteenth century and concerned the nature and virtue of traditional society. In *Gemeinschaft and Gesellschaft* (1887), Ferdinand Toennies argued that traditional society was based upon a web of implicit relationships that were fused and self-reinforcing. Close contact, shared values, and the unity of workplace and family life all contributed to a stable and integrated culture. Advancing industrialism caused a breakdown in this structure, with a resultant erosion of traditional virtues and values—a prospect Toennies viewed with alarm. Emile Durkheim, on the other hand, argued in "On Mechanical and Organic Solidarity" (1905) that the emerging pattern of social relations created its own kind of solidarity, one based upon explicit structures, information exchange, and role differentiation. Far from eliminating old virtues, such a structure allowed them to be perpetuated and elaborated in new, more fruitful ways. At stake in this argument, as noted by Laslett's *The World We Have Lost* (1965), is more than a faulty account of how things have changed. Our whole view of ourselves is altered based upon our belief that we have lost some more humane, much more natural pattern of relationships than that which modern society has to offer.

Arguments of similar kind increasingly seem to characterize discussions of American postsecondary education. Certainly, there exists no shortage of commentators to lament, in Laslett's words, "the world we have lost." Indeed, for many, the solution to achieving excellence in our current array of diverse institutions lies in a reaffirmation of traditional virtues: strong purpose, high standards, and a commitment to character typical of the small private institution of an earlier age (Martin 1982).

Such virtues are indeed important, and much can be learned by reexamining them. The operational question, however, is how such a reexamination can, in fact, take place. To expect a faculty in the complex environment of a large public research university, a multiconstituency community college, or a public regional service institution to practice such virtues simply because we tell them that such activities are valuable and traditional is surely not enough. We are not going to change the structures of what now constitute the majority of our institutions through pro-nouncement or exhortation. We need, rather, to build explicit administrative mechanisms, suited to the reality of our current institutions, to induce faculty and administrators to do what in a different setting they once did naturally.

Explicit, outcomes-oriented, institutional-assessment pro-cesses constitute one such mechanism, and one much more easily attainable than many now believe. Such assessment processes, like all formal accountability processes, have their dangers. In an era characterized by shrinking resources and greater public demands for short-term effectiveness, voluntary assessment on the part of colleges and universities constitutes an act of consider-able courage. Far from being irrational, institutional resistance to publicly evaluating institutional effectiveness is based on a real and historically justified apprehension that such processes will be misused by those outside the higher-education community. As

Durkheim warned about the emergence of explicit laws and roles in modernizing Europe, accountability structures can be oppressive as well as integrating.

But we may no longer have a choice. Public concerns for quality in higher education are real and persistent. Answering them will require that *all* institutions contribute. The challenge of the next decade will be to balance such concerns, legitimate though they may be, with a sensitivity for institutional differences and with a respect for participatory, faculty-centered decision-making. Explicit, institution-specific assessment processes can achieve such a balance, but only if they are implemented slowly, carefully, and with proper and constant reference to the ends of the enterprise—the vitality of the academic community and the students who inhabit it.

References

Astin, Alexander W. "Student Assessment." Working Paper prepared for the National Institute of Education [NIE] Study Group on the Conditions of Excellence in American Higher Education. NIE, Washington, D.C., 1984a.

———. "Theory of Student Involvement." Working Paper prepared for the Study Group on the Conditions of Excellence in American Higher Education. NIE, Washington, D.C., 1984b.

———. "Student Values: Knowing More About What We Are Today." *AAHE Bulletin* 36 (May 1984c):10-13.

———. "Student-Oriented Management: A Proposal for Change." In *Evaluating Educational Quality: A Conference Summary.* Washington, D.C.: Council on Postsecondary Accreditation, 1979.

Peter Ewell

———. *Four Critical Years: Effects of Colleges on Beliefs, Attitudes and Knowledge.* San Francisco: Jossey-Bass, 1977.

Astin, Alexander W.; Panos, R. J.; and Creager, J. A. *National Norms for Entering College Freshmen—Fall, 1966.* Washington, D.C.: American Council on Education, 1967.

Baldridge, J. Victor; Kemerer, Frank R.; and Green, Kenneth C. *Strategies for Effective Enrollment Management.* Washington, D.C.: American Association of State Colleges and Universities [AASCU], 1983.

Banta, Trudy W. "Final Report on the NCHEMS/Kellogg Student Outcomes Project at the University of Tennessee, Knoxville." University of Tennessee—Knoxville, 1984.

Barak, Robert J. *Program Review in Higher Education: Within and Without.* Boulder, Colo.: National Center for Higher Education Management Systems [NCHEMS], 1982.

Bloom, B. S., ed. *Taxonomy of Educational Objectives: Handbook 1: Cognitive Domain.* New York: David McKay, 1956.

Bogue, E. Grady. "Allocation of Public Funds on Institutional Performance/Quality Indicators." *International Journal of Institutional Management in Higher Education* 6 (March 1982):37-43.

Bogue, E. Grady, and Brown, Wayne. "Performance Incentives for State Colleges." *Harvard Business Review* 59 (November/December 1982):123-28.

Bowen, Howard R. *Investment in Learning: The Individual and Social Value of American Higher Education.* San Francisco: Jossey-Bass, 1977.

REFERENCES

Braskamp, Larry A. "Evaluation Systems Are More Than Information Systems." *Designing Academic Program Review*, pp. 55-66. New Directions for Higher Education, no. 37. Edited by R. Wilson. San Francisco: Jossey-Bass, 1982.

Chaffee, Ellen Earle. *After Decline, What? Survival Strategies at Eight Private Colleges*. Boulder, Colo.: NCHEMS, 1984.

Chickering, Arthur W. *Education and Identity*. San Francisco: Jossey-Bass, 1969.

Ewell, Peter T. "Institutional Uses of Student Outcomes Information." Final Report to the W. K. Kellogg Foundation on the NCHEMS/Kellogg Student Outcomes Project. NCHEMS, Boulder, Colo., 1984.

Ewell, Peter T., and Chaffee, Ellen Earle. "Promoting the Effective Use of Information in Decisionmaking." Paper presented at the 24th Annual Forum of the Association for Institutional Research, Ft. Worth, Texas, May 1984.

Eurich, A. C., and Pace, C. R. "A Follow-Up Study of Minnesota Graduates from 1928-1936." Committee on Educational Research, University of Minnesota, 1938.

Feldman, Kenneth A., and Newcomb, Theodore M. *The Impact of College on Students*. San Francisco: Jossey-Bass, 1969.

Feldman, Martha S., and March, James G. "Information in Organizations as Signal and Symbol." *Administrative Science Quarterly* 26 (1981):171-86.

Forrest, Aubrey W. *Increasing Student Competence and Persistence: The Best Case for General Education*. Iowa City, Iowa: American College Testing Program, 1982.

Peter Ewell

Forrest, Aubrey W., and Steele, Joe M. *College Outcome Measures Project.* Iowa City, Iowa: American College Testing Program, 1978.

Greenleaf, W. *Economic Status of College Alumni.* Bulletin 1937, no. 10. Washington, D.C.: U.S. Office of Education, 1939.

Harshman, Carl L. *A Model for Assessing the Quality of Non-Traditional Programs in Higher Education.* St. Louis: Metropolitan College, St. Louis University, 1979.

Learned, W. S., and Wood, B. D. *The Student and His Knowledge: A Report to the Carnegie Foundation on the Results of the High School and College Examinations of 1928, 1930 and 1932.* New York: Carnegie Foundation for the Advancement of Teaching, 1938.

Lenning, Oscar T. *The Outcomes Structure: An Overview and Procedures for Applying It in Postsecondary Institutions.* Boulder, Colo.: NCHEMS, 1977a.

————. *Previous Attempts to Structure Educational Outcomes and Outcome-Related Concepts.* Boulder, Colo.: NCHEMS, 1977b.

Lenning, Oscar, and Munday, Leo. *The Many Faces of College Success and Their Nonintellective Correlates: The Published Literature Through the Decade of the Sixties.* Iowa City, Iowa: American College Testing Program, 1974.

Martin, Warren Bryan. *A College of Character.* San Francisco: Jossey-Bass, 1982.

Matthews, Jana B., and Norgaard, Rolf. *Managing the Partnership Between Higher Education and Industry.* Boulder, Colo.: NCHEMS, 1984.

REFERENCES

McClain, Charles J. *Degrees of Integrity: A Value Added Approach with Undergraduate Assessment.* Washington, D.C.: AASCU, 1984.

————. "Evidences of the Effectiveness and Success of the Value-Added Program." Northeast Missouri State University, Kirksville, Mo., April 1983.

Mentkowski, Marcia, and Doherty, Austin. *Careering After College: Establishing the Validity of Abilities Learned in College for Later Careering and Professional Performance.* Milwaukee, Wis.: Alverno College, 1984.

National Institute of Education. *Involvement in Learning.* Report of the Study Group on the Conditions of Excellence in American Higher Education. Washington, D.C.: Government Printing Office, 1984.

Newcomb, T. M.; Koenig, K; Flacks, R.; and Warwick, D. D. *Persistence and Change: Bennington College and Its Students After Twenty-Five Years.* New York: John Wiley and Sons, 1967.

Pace, C. Robert. *Measuring the Quality of College Student Experiences.* Los Angeles: Higher Education Research Institute, University of California at Los Angeles, 1984.

————. "Historical Perspectives on Student Outcomes Assessment with Implications for the Future." Paper presented at the 65th Annual Conference of the National Association of Student Personnel Administrators, Toronto, Canada, April 1983.

————. *Measuring the Outcomes of College.* San Francisco: Jossey-Bass, 1979.

————. *The Demise of Diversity?* Berkeley, Calif.: Carnegie Commission on Higher Education, 1974.

Peter Ewell

Sheldon, M. Stephen. *Statewide Longitudinal Study: Report on Academic Year 1978-81*. Final Report. Los Angeles: Los Angeles Pierce College, 1981.

Sheldon, M. Stephen, and Grafton, Clife L. "Raison d'Etre: Students." *Community and Junior College Journal* 53 (November 1982):19-20.

Spaeth, J. L., and Greeley, A. M. *Recent Alumni and Higher Education*. New York: McGraw-Hill, 1970.

Trent, J. W., and Medsker, L. *Beyond High School: A Psychosociological Study of 10,000 High School Graduates*. San Francisco: Jossey-Bass, 1968.

Trivett, David A. *Proprietary Schools and Postsecondary Education*. ERIC Higher Education Research Report, no. 2. Washington, D.C.: American Association for Higher Education, 1974.

Walleri, R. Dan. "Student Retention and Attrition in the Community College: A Review and Research Design." Arlington, Va.: ERIC Document Reproduction Service, ED 210064, 1981.

The NCHEMS
Executive Overview Series

The books in the Executive Overview Series are available at $10.00 each plus 50¢ per copy for shipping and handling.

Order Form

Please send me the following Executive Overviews at $10.00 each:

QTY.	TITLE	PRICE

Plus 50¢ per book for shipping and handling

TOTAL

Name _____ Title _____

Department _____ Institution _____

Address _____ City _____ State _____ Zip _____

☐ Payment Enclosed
(Make checks payable to NCHEMS)

☐ Charge Institutional P.O. # _____
(Enclose Purchase Order with this form)

Return to:
NCHEMS Publications Department • P.O. Drawer P • Boulder, CO 80303
Or Call (303) 497-0390

02820127000401
2M:185:LP:D&K:2BA369